ROAD TO RECOVERY

Growth and Change

PERSONAL STORIES BY PEOPLE WHO'VE BEEN THERE

EDITED BY DALE H.
FOREWORD BY DR. ROBERT J. ACKERMAN

PUBLISHED BY THE RENASCENT FOUNDATION

Copyright

Growth and Change

Copyright © 2015 Renascent Foundation Inc.

All rights reserved. No part of this book may be used or reproduced by any means, graphic, electronic, or mechanical, including photocopying, recording, taping or by any information storage retrieval system without the written permission of the publisher except in the case of brief quotations embodied in critical articles and reviews.

Library and Archives Canada Cataloguing in Publication

Growth and Change / edited by Dale H.

Issued in print and electronic formats.

ISBN 978-0-9947998-2-1 (paperback).--ISBN 978-0-9947998-3-8 (ebook)

1. Alcoholics--Rehabilitation.

I. H., Dale, 1957-, editor

HV5278.G76 2015   616.86'106   C2015-904947-4

C2015-904948-2

Cover by Jacques Pilon Design Communications

Print format by Chris G.

Published by Renascent Foundation Inc.

Dedication

This is book is dedicated to ...

the thousands of men, women and children who've found recovery through Renascent. Your recovery stories let others know that recovery is possible and beautiful — even in the face of challenges that once may have seemed insurmountable.

our Guardian Angels and all of our donors, small and large — who support recovery by making charitable gifts to the Renascent Foundation. With donors by our side, cost is removed as a barrier for the majority who seek help but cannot afford to pay.

Acknowledgements

Editor: Dale H.

Publishing Facilitator: Roger C.

Editorial Committee: Anne P., Caroline L., Dale H., Jeff C., Petra M., Roger C.

Proofreader: Christine Sanger

Renascent Foundation Project Manager: Joanne Steel

Published by Renascent Foundation Inc.
Lillian and Don Wright Family Health Centre
38 Isabella Street, Toronto, ON M4Y 1N1
Charitable #11911 5434 RR0001

24/7 Recovery Helpline: 1-866-232-1212

www.renascent.ca

Table of Contents

Foreword 1
Introduction 3
To My Beautiful Brothers and Sisters Who Struggle 7
A Letter to Alcohol 11
Great Expectations 15
How Do I Feel? 19
I Needed Help as Much as He Did 21
Getting Out of My Head 23
Overcoming the Fear 27
The "A" Word 31
The Gift of Self-esteem 33
Shame and Guilt Affect Family Members, Too 37
A New Freedom 41
The Detective's Gift 45
Sobriety 102 49
It's a Good Day to be Sober 53
We Have Our Daughter Back 57
Now What? 59
The New Normal 63
My Wish for You is a Billy M 65
Catching Volunteer Fever 67
I'm Okay ... You're Okay 69
Spiralling Up 73
A True Partnership 75
Tiny Speck, Infinite Power 77
So Just ... Give Up 79
It Was Time to Stop Waiting 83
Brand New All Over Again 87
Why Gratitude Makes Me Happy 91
In the Footsteps of My Father 95
No Secrets, No Lies, No Excuses 97
It's an Inside Job 101
Trusting the Voice Inside 105

Learning to Start Living Again..107
A Journey to Myself..109
We Are Not a Glum Lot..113
Recovery Love...117
That's Progress!..119
A Mugful of Humility...121
"Non-doing" is Hard to Do!..125
"Face Everything And Recover"...129
A Man in Need of a Psychic Change......................................133
To Thine Own Self Be True...137
From Amorphous Me to Authentic Me.................................141
Peeking Through Joy's Window..145
Time Out...149
Painting my Life with Colour..151
About Renascent..155

Foreword

When we attempt to change our thinking and our behaviours, how do we know if we are getting better? I remember asking a person working on his sobriety, "How are you doing?" He replied, "I go to meetings" and I asked, "How are you doing?" He said, "I go to a lot of meetings." Again, I repeated, "How are you doing?" He asked, "Do you think I should go to more meetings?" Finally, I said, "Well, I know what you do with your time, but how are you doing?"

Whether spoken or unspoken, recovery should have goals. As you read the following stories, you'll notice the goals for each person become clearer as his or her acceptance of reality and desire for a better life become stronger. We might start a journey with only one goal, such as sobriety, but as we achieve success, we begin to realize that there are many benefits to sobriety. In fact, the goals of a recovering person might be:

- to make better decisions in our lives and to make responsible choices
- to develop healthy social behaviours
- to improve our relationships with family and friends
- to follow our recovery plan
- to live a clean and sober life every day

This last goal is the most important. It is the one that truly tells us that not only have we changed, but also that we have changed for the better. It tells us that we now talk the talk, walk the walk, and take the steps.

As I read these stories, a few other things about growth and change became obvious. For example, after all of the hard work to bring about change, we should celebrate our recovery. Live it. Enjoy it. Love it. Share it. Every 12-step meeting is a celebration of the healthy choices we are making.

Learning to live without fear is vital to our growth. After all, when we meet new challenges, we now have a recovery plan. Living a balanced life means we are no longer controlling nor do we wish to control others. Changes give us the opportunity to like ourselves, not in a narcissistic way, but rather in a self-respecting one. It is an unrealistic dream to expect other people to like us and love us when we don't even like what we have to offer.

I have learned that the greatest barrier to change is the inability to receive help from others and the inability to receive the benefits of recovery. There are many causes of this inability, but not realizing that we have choices is a significant one. I know, for example, that "Yes, I am an adult child of an alcoholic, and I will be a child of an alcoholic until the day I die, but I am not going to die one more day because I am an adult child of an alcoholic." We do have choices.

Dr. Robert J. Ackerman

Bluffton, SC

USA

Introduction

My name is Dale and I am an alcoholic.

Twenty years ago, I said these words to a roomful of women in Walker House, Renascent's treatment centre for women at that time. I certainly didn't want to be there. But somewhere under the fog of my alcoholism, at my very bottom, I knew that I needed to be there. I had nowhere else to go.

Over the next 28 days, I would say those same words again and again. I would listen as the other women shared their pain, their fear, their anger, their shame and confusion. I would learn just what alcoholism was and why I could not drink "normally." Most importantly, I would learn that there was a solution, that there was hope, that recovery was indeed possible. Renascent has continued to be a touchstone in my personal journey of recovery throughout the years. I can never repay what they so freely and lovingly gave me.

Ten years ago, I was asked to guest edit a few issues of the Renascent alumni newsletter, *TGIF Weekly Recovery News*. Little did I know that today I'd be looking back on a decade of work as the newsletter's editor and have the joy of seeing the writers' contributions evolve into an anthology series of print and e-books.

TGIF was created in 2000 by Renascent Alumni Coordinator Lisa North as an innovative means of strengthening and supporting our far-flung alumni community by using the then rather cutting-edge technology of email and web browsers. In keeping with the 12-step tradition of storytelling, the newsletter (initially named *tiktalk*) largely consisted of Lisa's weekly reflections on recovery, supplemented by announcements of alumni events and sobriety anniversaries. The newsletter slowly evolved to contain interviews, relevant news stories and the occasional personal essay written by Renascent alumni, and was renamed *TGIF*.

Under the helm of Alumni Coordinator Charles McMulkin, *TGIF* evolved into an engaging, relevant and topical newsletter featuring lived experience essays written by Renascent alumni, coupled with contributions by professionals in the addiction and recovery field. During Joanne Steel's tenure, the voices of family members were strengthened and friends in the broader recovery community were invited to contribute their personal stories of recovery as well.

The juxtaposition of the didactic and the personal continues to be the foundation of TGIF. Videos, book reviews, poetry, special issues and Renascent outreach initiatives have all been added. But the heart of TGIF remains the personal stories told by alumni and others in recovery, from the newly sober to the long-timer.

Today, TGIF Weekly Recovery News reaches thousands of subscribers each week via email. All content also resides in our TGIF blog on the Renascent website (www.renascent.ca). Go have a look. There are over 1,000 articles and essays on just about any aspect of recovery you can imagine. Subscribe to TGIF while you're there!

As the editor of TGIF, I have long believed that these beautiful stories of recovery deserved a broader platform. Enter Joanne Steel, Renascent's Manager of Major Gifts and Communications. With Joanne's customary drive, passion and tenacity, these anthologies finally turned from dream into reality. Our volunteer editorial committee members spent hours poring through essays, looking to find the gems that best represent the limitless opportunities for growth offered to us as we live and learn in recovery.

The book you're holding features the experience, strength and hope of men and women who are living the reality of recovery each and every day. To them, we give our deepest thanks for their honesty and willingness to share their stories, their challenges and their victories as they walk the road of recovery with courage.

The "God question" has often presented a challenge to newcomers to 12-step recovery. Program literature makes it clear that the road to a spiritual awakening is a broad one, yet this essential truth can somehow get lost in translation. This volume reflects the experience of our writers: that spirituality can be experienced in any number of different ways.

You'll read stories of people of different religious faiths or none at all, atheists, agnostics, those who embrace other spiritual traditions, those who find their higher power in a higher purpose or through their creative spirit. All these voices and more are a chorus of hope and encouragement that you too can tap into "an unsuspected inner resource" on your own journey of recovery.

Essays written by Renascent alumni indicate the Renascent house they attended and the year they went through treatment. Contributions by our friends in the broader recovery community are identified by name alone. Renascent uses the 12-step treatment model (in conjunction with other treatment modalities) and, in accordance with the tradition of anonymity, all writers are identified by first name and last initial only.

To My Beautiful Brothers and Sisters Who Struggle ...

Paul S. (Punanai 2011)

To my beautiful brothers and sisters who struggle ...

... know that you are never alone. While you may feel that no one could possibly be in more pain, in more trouble or more desperate than you ... there are countless of us who have been there and know what you are going through. Grab the hand that reaches for you, for it desires to help you beyond measure.

To my beautiful brothers and sisters who struggle ...

... see that powerlessness and surrender do not mean weakness. Strength comes from our ability to see that we need help and that our struggle to control things is only a wasted effort. When we give our will and our lives over to the care of a Higher Power, we are tapping into a power — a power that is beyond measure.

To my beautiful brothers and sisters who struggle ...

... recognize that you are a sick person getting well, not a bad person getting good. Our actions may have been poor and our judgment lacking during our drinking days, but no one has the right to make us feel less than. You are finding the path to wellness and recovery — and the joy a life of sobriety brings is beyond measure.

To my beautiful brothers and sisters who struggle ...

... learn that you are worthy of everything wonderful that is due to you. You have worth in this world, and you are needed by us. Your light is unique, your talents one-of-a-kind and your capacity to grow is limitless. Your usefulness in this world is beyond measure.

To my beautiful brothers and sisters who struggle ...

... do this only for you and you alone. Do not take this on for anyone other than you. To do so is futile. Many lives have been lost in the name of appeasement and kowtowing. Recovery is an act that may at first seem selfish, but is selfless ever more. Being true to what the Creator meant us to be, sober, is a gift to others that is beyond measure.

To my beautiful brothers and sisters who struggle ...

... remember that your life was not always like this. You had interests — things that captured your imagination and captivated your spirit, that made the music in your soul ring loudly throughout your life. Drinking killed ambition and took you away from you. Transforming your life takes time, but is a journey that is beyond measure.

To my beautiful brothers and sisters who struggle ...

... be aware that wherever you go, you are there. We cannot escape ourselves as much as we cannot escape gravity. You are uncovering your inner beauty through stripping away what doesn't serve you. You are removing the grime that took the shine off your once glimmering soul; a soul whose purpose is to gleam onto others in ways that are beyond measure.

To my beautiful brothers and sisters who struggle ...

... know that alcohol is not the problem, but the solution. And a poor solution at that to what ails us, which is essentially mental, physical and spiritual in nature. Not being able to touch our own skin from within drives us to try and plug the God-sized hole inside for years and years. And it never works. That need for love and acceptance within us that we find in Him is quenched beyond measure.

To my beautiful brothers and sisters who struggle ...

... understand that things get worse, and never better. But no matter how far down the scale you go, there is always hope. There is always a chance to catch the old fire of our spirits that were dulled by the thoughts in our mind, the bottle and the ego that told us that next time, things will be different. The power of delusional thinking is dangerous beyond measure.

To my beautiful brothers and sisters who struggle ...

... see that you weren't meant to suffer the way you suffer. We weren't meant to hurt and be hurt the way we have. We weren't created to feel that life would be better if we just escaped through death by our own hand. We weren't put on this earth to plunge solely into darkness. The amount of freedom and relief we can find in recovery is beyond measure.

To my beautiful brothers and sisters who struggle ...

A Letter to Alcohol

Barb L. (Munro 1997)

My dearest, most dangerous friend,

We have been inseparable partners for many years, but the time has come to say goodbye. You were once my saviour. Now, you are my devastation. My dependence upon you has created a raging sickness in my body and soul; thus, we must part.

Ours was a case of love at first sight. You brought me to a place of comfort and warmth, and equipped me with self-esteem and a persona. Insecurity magically disappeared and was replaced with a sense of power and ease. I felt at home in a strange world where I once had no place. Without you, I felt awkward, ugly and stupid. With you, I appeared to be together, comfortably social, a leader — someone that people admired.

Our "love" quickly flourished over the years. I drank your energy when I was feeling inadequate, tired or lonely. Of course, I also drank to celebrate — absolutely anything. I was exciting and outrageous. I enjoyed being the first in the crowd to try anything. I revelled in my uniqueness. Being around me was definitely an adventure. To my amazement, some even envied me. Little did they know what was happening inside. You had messed up my mind to such a degree that I didn't even know myself.

Eventually, things changed — you turned on me. I don't remember when, exactly. The greatest gift you had given me was the ability to escape from the incessant void I felt in my soul. For the longest time, I could ignore and internalize all the chaos. Unfortunately, the turmoil began to crack through the surface of my not-so-thick shell and ooze out into all areas of my life. I lost all control — over my emotions, my actions and most of all, over you. You called to me constantly ...

"Drink me ... drink me ... all the anxiety will disappear ... swallow me into your soul ... I will fill your void. I will make you whole."

The more I drank you, the less I could experience life. More and more came the terrifying, dark moments. In them, I was watching myself through glass in some kind of wretched film and I had no control over the ending.

I had become a liar, a thief, a bad friend. I hated other women who seemed to be what I desperately wished I were. I hated myself. I chose unhealthy relationships because in life, we attract what we are. I pushed away the people that saw the goodness in me, and who loved me for who I really was. Eventually, I desired only to be around people that loved you as much as I. It became obvious that normal, sane people did not need you like I did. They could take you or leave you. I could not. And so I became more removed from reality, and from people. I began to go out alone, so I could drink you with other lost souls. We had nothing in common, other than our mutual friend in a deadly bottle.

I began to fear meeting people "outside" that I had met with you, as I would often have only vague or no recollection whatsoever of having made their acquaintance. I dreaded hearing of the horrible things that I had done with you that I could not remember. The next day, any evidence of our adventures sent a cold shiver down my spine. My life had become like a black hole, pulling me inside its emptiness — into darkness, further and further. The time finally came when I had to hide out with you so people wouldn't know my secret, and so I wouldn't have to worry about my actions. It was you and me against the world, obliterating the stark reality of life.

I had known for a long time that I was becoming more and more dependent upon you. I just ignored it, in hopes that life would somehow magically get better. When things got to their lowest point ever, I realized that something had to be done; the insanity was too great. I could not live like that; yet I was too afraid to die.

Desperate and alone, I walked into a meeting of Alcoholics Anonymous. Suddenly, I became awake. The people showed me that you could no longer live vicariously through me if I chose life instead. They shared stories of their battles with you, and inspired my soul.

Friend, you robbed me of 14 years of my life. I will not to allow you to steal any more of my precious time.

Living without you is a process of hard work, of deep introspection and healing of a dying spirit. I now have a chance to discover the life for which I am destined, that I once chose to ignore. I don't have to do it all alone any longer. There is finally a way to fight the obsession that I have had for you over the years, and continue to have every single day.

For the first time, I can accept the help of people who show me that beauty lives deep inside of me. Although I still do not know who that "me" is yet, I am confident that she will slowly come to life again. I am sick and tired of living on the edge and blindly walking in circles when there are so many wonderful things in store for me. I am tired of failure, meaninglessness and unfinished tasks. I am sick of depending upon luck alone. I want to be proud of my accomplishments and growth rather than feeling constant shame and remorse.

It is time to say goodbye, fatal friend. You are the devil to me, and have cunningly led me away from the goodness and beauty of life. I will fight you on a daily basis, with the help of people, a power greater than myself and a power greater than you. I will do what is required of me to keep me out of your captivity, and to make up for the harm I have caused myself and others. They have told me the promises are there for those who want it. I want it, badly.

Goodbye. Good riddance. I pray for your victims who have not yet discovered your evil seeping into their lives. I hope one day to be sane enough to help save someone else from his or her inevitable destruction.

Great Expectations

Tokio (Munro 2009)

When I take an Advil for a headache, I *expect* the headache to go away. The "solution" I have just swallowed is *expected* to solve my problem of pain. When I pay my rent every month, I *expect* to be able to keep living in my apartment. When you hurt me, I *expect* an apology and when I screw up, I *expect* you to forgive me.

These are everyday things for me. My life is full of *life* and hence riddled with *expectations* ... sometimes *great expectations* ... *elephant-sized expectations*. Like when I went to rehab, I *expected* to be cured. And so did my family.

We were all so pregnant with *expectation* that it seemed there would be no chance of failure. Relief from this awful alcoholism would be delivered in 21 days. We all thought all I had to do was just stay in rehab and the alcohol problem would be solved.

The problem was that *I* was the problem and I was 43 years old ... you can't solve 43 years old with 21 new days.

We know that now, but back then when I picked up a drink 72 hours after leaving rehab, it was devastating. That one liquid drink smashed my expectations like a solid iron sledgehammer ... maybe that's why they call it "getting hammered."

You see, I *expected* everything to add up. And things might have if I had done something besides time. I *expected* something for nothing. I sat in a chair in the places I was told to go and I opened my mouth but kept my ears and mind locked up like Fort Knox. I made no effort to understand or participate and I *expected* my efforts to be banked. And they were — I put zero effort in and I got zero sobriety back. In actual fact, I did get something out of it ... I got drunk.

It took four years to figure out that by doing some work as opposed to having expectations, I could make capital gains in my recovery. I can leave the bars and the "rapacious creditor" of alcoholism and go where we exchange the currency of "The Bank of Bill and Bob." What I get to gain is "interest in others." What I get to save is my relationship with my daughter. And there are no service fees. I'm just given the opportunity to do service so I can keep what I've gained and saved. It's a sweet deal. I challenge you to find a better one.

One of the perks that comes with this deal for me, and anyone who is willing to go to any lengths, is the relationship with a sponsor. I couldn't stay sober until I got one that I was willing to work with. Several agreed to work with me but I wasn't willing. I wasn't ready yet to become willing to be willing to be willing ... I hadn't lost enough *yet*.

"Yet" arrived in the form of losing everything I cared about: my marriage, my relationships with my daughter and my family, my house, my career, and my friends. When I lost enough, I became more than willing to shut my mouth and open my heart and mind. And especially open my ears. And into my open ears, my sponsor deposited the words "expectations are resentments waiting to happen."

I had expected so much of people and they let me down. And I had, many times over, returned the favour. Then, one day in a meeting, I heard someone say, "people will let you down ... that's just what they do."

I was shocked. I mean, I know that concept as a reality and experience, but in my family, you are a pure failure and plain stupid if you let others down. That "letting down" of something besides your hair becomes family legend, and tales are told of your failure around the fire. As a sensitive alcoholic, this story time was torture, as I was often the main character.

But by chance or heredity, I'm an alcoholic and by destiny, I'm lucky enough to be in the rooms and my ears have been opened by the force of pain. The soothing words of "people will let you down ... that's just what they do" pour in.

And those words are followed by, "people are always just doing the best they can." Double wow. So even when I'm screwing up and you're flipping out, we are both just doing the best we can. What a relief. Way better than Advil for a headache or alcohol for a heartache. I no longer have to expect you to do anything but the best you can. I no longer have to resent you because you are doing the best you can ... And so am I.

How Do I Feel?

Roger C.

When I went to rehab in 2010, it didn't feel like I walked through the doors at the main entrance. It felt like I crawled under those doors.

I didn't know what I was doing there. I didn't know what had happened. But I knew I had somehow committed myself to staying for three weeks. I didn't understand that, either.

I got used to the routines. Nothing too complicated. Every morning at 6:30 a.m., we would all trundle down to the gym and do some exercises while listening to loud music. Then we would go outside and walk for a mile or so. After a while, I enjoyed starting my day that way. After the walk, we would have to check in.

There was a lot of checking in. We would have to stop everything and get together with our group and "check in" with a counsellor three times a day.

One of the questions asked at check-in was, "How do you feel?"

Three times a day, "How do you feel?"

I found the question a bit odd, to say the least. And there were rules about how you could answer the question. You weren't allowed to say, for example, "fine." Apparently that meant something like "Effed-up Interior, Nice Exterior." Once I learned what it meant, I always wanted to answer, "Fine." I thought it described me pretty well. At least the interior part.

There was even a sheet that they handed out that had a list of ways a person could feel, and could answer the question. A list of 30 or 40 possible feelings! Can you imagine? With emoticons, or whatever they're called. When asked, "How do you feel?" the answer had to be one of these, and never, ever, the word "fine."

So I dealt with this for about a week. Twenty times or so, they asked me how I felt.

Finally, I was in my group in the middle of the afternoon and a counsellor asked me the dreaded question. I had had enough.

I let her rip, shouting at the top of my lungs: "Feelings? Feelings? Haven't you people been listening? Haven't you heard my story? I've been drinking for 40 years. I don't have feelings!"

For a few seconds, there was a stunned silence. Then my roommate, Daniel, started laughing. And then others joined in. Finally, everybody was laughing, roaring really, including the counsellor. I looked at these people around me, people I had gotten to know at least a little since entering rehab, and I did something I hadn't done yet there:

I smiled.

The next few weeks went by pretty quickly. Mostly the counsellors would smile when they asked how I felt, and I would smile back. Sometimes, I would answer by picking a feeling from the list on the sheet, but every time I was asked, I would stop to think about it.

"How do I feel?" I would ask myself.

In recovery, I have learned to look at my feelings. To feel my feelings. To understand that I have them, to recognize and acknowledge them.

And I have learned that it is okay to have nice feelings; even to nurture them. I can have good feelings about myself and about others. Imagine! I wasn't too good about caring for others before but I have been giving it a try over the past few years and it is amazing to me how just that — trying to care about others and sometimes succeeding — has changed how I live, day to day, moment to moment.

How do I feel?

I may have crawled under the doors to get into rehab but if someone had asked me how I felt as I walked out after completing treatment, I would have answered, truthfully, "I feel hope."

And so it has been ever since.

I Needed Help as Much as He Did

Mary H. (Family Program)

My experience with addiction treatment was not at all what I'd expected. I had gone with my husband to the treatment centre to inquire about it, because I'd reached the end of my rope; I'd left him, and wouldn't return unless he received treatment and stopped drinking. A simple request, I thought. I was tired of constantly walking on eggshells, the constant worrying. He reluctantly agreed, and we walked through the doors of recovery on that fateful day.

But when my husband stepped away with someone to discuss treatment, I was surprised by the approach of a friendly face. Her eyes were full of warmth and assurance. Why was she interested in speaking with *me*? *I* wasn't the one who needed help, *he was*! I was taken to another room where we discussed my life at home. I poured my heart out, and felt much better afterward. I was told that recovery is important for the entire family, not just the addict. How naïve I was, that I didn't realize that I needed help as much as he did!

In recovery, I learned that I am not alone. Many people are touched by the effects of alcoholism and addiction. Hearing how others deal with their pain successfully (or sometimes unsuccessfully) continually helps me to make educated decisions about my own life.

One of the greatest gifts that I received in recovery is knowledge. Understanding the disease of alcoholism has allowed me to build compassion for my alcoholic. We need compassion to achieve loving detachment, which is one of the most powerful methods of self-care.

Taking care of myself may or may not change my alcoholic's behaviour, but it has certainly changed my life. It helped me to bring the focus on myself, rather than incessantly stressing over whether or not he's drinking, and how he'll behave after having a few too many. It also taught me about personal boundaries, that I don't need to be living in an environment that could be potentially dangerous. I didn't leave because I wanted to punish him; I left because I did what was right for me, a concept that had eluded me for many years.

The weekly meetings, or "classes," as I like to call them, taught me about the symptoms of alcoholism. I'd previously believed that my loved one had a character flaw, and saw his behaviour as lazy and irresponsible. I have now come to understand that these are symptoms of the disease, and not his personality.

I most certainly do not excuse his behaviour; I have just come to an understanding that when promises aren't kept, I can accept and move on, rather than dwell on disappointment. Before, I would get angry, have an argument, and in the end we would both be unhappy. I've now learned to accept, move on and make other plans. Life goes on. I need not rely on someone else to make me happy — I can take responsibility for my own happiness. Acceptance has played a huge part in my recovery.

One of the most freeing benefits of recovery is learning to allow my husband the dignity to make his own mistakes. It is not my responsibility to constantly protect him, to call his work when he is sick, etc. I used to fret over what would happen, and felt compelled to "fix" everything to make it right. What I didn't realize was that this did the exact opposite of what I'd intended to do. I'd never allowed him to learn the natural consequences of his mistakes, and therefore I was enabling him to continue to drink.

I've come a long way since I began my road to recovery in this past year. I learned to forgive, and to see hope in the future. I love my husband and hate the addiction. Continually learning to cope with the effects of alcoholism has strengthened me and has given me the courage to change my life in a positive way. I am forever grateful to have been given the opportunity for my own recovery.

Getting Out of My Head

Felix V. (Punanai 2006)

I don't think I'm the first person to have this thought in their first 30 days of sitting in yet another dank church basement: "Is this really what my life has come to?"

What I told myself was this: "I am willing to forever give up having fun if it means never having to experience the hell of active addiction again." This time I was honestly done and willing to give this thing called "recovery" a shot.

I was okay with the fact that meetings and ruing my existence would be the basic menu of my reality for the rest of my life. Oh, well. It was a fitting end to what I thought was a life cursed from the beginning. At least now I had some people to listen to me whine.

They were very nice to me and just kind of laughed under their breath as I moaned and complained, and they told me to "keep coming back." I mean, they were pleasant and all, but so fake with those smiles and talking about being "grateful" and "happy." I figured that instead of participating or getting involved, I'd just sit there in the back corner, try to calm my nervous shaking and keep a safe distance from them.

Still pretty much deaf, dumb and blind to the suggestions I was hearing from others, one night I somehow took the remarkable step of staying after the meeting and putting some chairs away. It was getting close to my 30 days and I was discovering that I was, in many ways, profoundly more crazy sober than when I was using. Those damn voices in my head just wouldn't shut up!

Certainly, going home to my parents (who had begrudgingly taken me in yet one more time) wasn't going to make those voices any quieter. Might as well stay for a bit, put some chairs away, and at least be in the presence of people who didn't sit there gazing at me with a mixture of disgust and fear.

It was while putting those cruddy chairs away that an old-timer approached me and said, "Looks like you're pretty stuck in your head." I looked back at him with that quintessential newcomer look that simply says, "Huh?" That's when he said something that would help change my life. "You know, the most dangerous place on earth for me is between my ears. You see, there ain't no adult supervision up there."

For some reason, that line affected me like it was the funniest thing I had ever heard. It had been years since I had laughed that hard. It was the laugh of identification. The laugh was belly-filled, and snowballed up from my stomach until I was on the ground, my eyes tearing up from it. There on that dirty floor, curled with my knees to my chest, I realized what it meant to be out of my head. "Putting these chairs away is about the best thing you can do," the old-timer told me. "There's nothing better for getting outside of yourself than service."

I had actually hated that word, "service," when I first heard it in the rooms of AA. The whole making coffee thing just seemed ridiculous to me. Those little things people said to do — put up chairs, help clean up, make coffee — struck me as trivial and insignificant. I mean, I was here to get sober and change my life, not to run to the store to get cream for the coffee. But soon after that old-timer had me in stitches on the floor, I was arriving at the meeting early to help set up.

On one such morning I met the person who would become my first sponsor. I joined a group. I also started going to business meetings. Then a really weird thing happened: I started taking ownership for the cleanliness and overall presentation of my group. I was helping the secretary order chips. (God forbid we had a newcomer and no 24-hour chips!) And if someone was new, I made sure to put out my hand and welcome that person. And, yes, I probably became a little more possessive over the coffeemaker than was healthy. But, God darn it, people deserve a good cup of coffee at a meeting and it was up to me to make it for them.

I would love to say that I took that ethic of service outside of the rooms with me right away, but I didn't. I guess I was still too bitter and resentful at my life and those around me. My poor parents had to put up with my attitude for three more months until I went into Renascent and then recovery housing.

It took 12 steps, hard work and the help of my higher power to eventually get me to the point where I was actually pleasant to be around. Service in the rooms, especially in those early days, was about the only real solution I had for those voices in my head that were driving me crazy.

Almost four years later, I still hold it as an essential truth for me: service makes me feel better. This is now as true for me outside the rooms as it is inside. I honestly look for opportunities where I can be helpful. And I do it for me.

Please have no doubts: as much as I might seem an upstanding member of society today, there remains, to this very day, absolutely no adult supervision between my ears. Spending too much time alone up there is as dangerous to me now as it ever has been. In giving back, I help myself way more than anyone who might benefit from what I do for them.

Overcoming the Fear

Nevada T. (Munro 2013)

Let's start off with a couple of recovery definitions of FEAR: F*** Everything And Run or Face Everything And Recover. And let's face it, before we step into recovery, our lives are driven by some sort of fear. A fear of success, failure, responsibility, anything, and we lack a better solution than drugs.

Some of us may know why we use and some may not. No matter what, we reach a certain point in our addiction where we come to realize that we cannot stay clean on our own, and we need some help. To begin the journey, many of us choose to attend a treatment centre. In today's day and age, there is a lot of stigma around addiction.

Some are afraid to speak out to loved ones, bosses or friends that they have a problem because they will be forever labelled as an addict or an alcoholic. This makes taking the initiative to get into treatment quite the challenge. There are others whose addiction is known, and others who are forced to get help. Whatever the back story is, we are all hesitant to take those simple but huge steps into the unknown.

Living life leaning on a bottle or a drug for support is the only way many of us know how to live. Either we never knew or we forget how to live and enjoy life as a normal human being. Whatever "normal" may be.

To finally face reality and admit we have a problem and to do something to get better is a challenging feat, especially when we don't know what to expect. Thankfully, before I entered treatment, I had been told that it was the best thing I would ever do for myself. Some may be skeptical because they have heard some treatment horror stories, or because they've never heard anything at all. Let me be the one to tell you, it was truly the best thing I ever did for myself.

During the preceding weeks to my admission date, I was feeling a mixture of emotions that would usually lead me to use — fear, anxiety, excitement, shame, guilt, etc. I felt like I was starting the rest of my life, and it was nerve-racking to say the least.

When the day finally came, I walked into Renascent feeling miserable and extremely awkward. My plan was to keep my head down and survive the 21 days. I kept on hearing this term "open-mindedness"; something extremely foreign to me since I lived in this bubble surrounded by drugs and alcohol for so long.

I didn't know what else was out there, and I didn't really think this whole treatment thing was going to work for me. I expected that while I was there, the counsellors were going to nit-pick my life and push religion on me and then I would be "cured." Boy, was I ever wrong.

Before going into treatment, I thought I was different than everybody else — looked down upon in society — and would never be accepted. When I walked into that treatment centre, the first thing I learned was that addiction can impact anyone, no matter what sex, age, race or religion. Within the first hour, I felt more comfortable there than I had ever felt anywhere else in my life. I was surrounded by people who were exactly like me.

They explained to me that we would have structure and that there were certain rules I would have to follow. Being the person I am, I rebelled against it all for the first week, only to realize that I was causing myself more harm than good, and that there must be a reason behind what the counsellors were telling me to do. Honesty, open-mindedness and willingness were the three key terms. Once I accepted where I was, and that this place was there to help me, I gained the knowledge and got the push I needed to really embrace recovery.

During the second week, I finally started to believe there was hope. We had two classes a day in which we would dissect the Steps of Alcoholics Anonymous and share honestly and openly with the other residents based on the chosen topic. Unbeknownst to me at the time, the class followed the guidelines of a closed 12-step meeting.

It was also the time where I really got to know my fellow addicts. I learned the necessary tools through these classes to repair and maintain a healthy relationship, and got started working on it right away.

I was petrified to bring up what I had done in the past because of my addiction and what had happened prior to influence my actions. When I overcame the fear, the counsellors and my peers embraced me with open arms, comforted me and reassured me I was not alone.

I'm not trying to make it sound like it was always easy; there were days I didn't want to get out of bed, let alone talk about my feelings. But that's life. There will always be struggles and feelings of unease and discomfort. The difference between me in active addiction and me after treatment is how I cope with those feelings.

I had thought for awhile in treatment that the counsellors were full of themselves, and that they didn't know how I felt. The reality of the situation is that they did, and they've been there, and they are in recovery. They use their experience to benefit each and every one of us that enter through the doors. I walked out of treatment with a new view on life; one filled with hope, Twelve Steps and recovery.

I'm not perfect to this day and never will be; something else I learned in Renascent. But as long as I use what they taught me, I will stay clean and be the best me I can possibly be.

Keep in mind the wise words of Eleanor Roosevelt — "You gain strength, courage and confidence by every experience in which you really stop to look fear in the face."

The "A" Word

Paul S. (Punanai 2011)

I was at a bookstore some time ago, perusing the titles in the alcoholism and addiction section. Two teenage girls nearby started to rifle through the shelves until they got to where I was standing. Upon discovering the topics of the books, one of the girls turned to the other, and with a hint of disdain in her voice, announced, "Oh, those books are for alkies."

Now, I don't have an issue with the terms "alkie," "drunk," "booze pig," etc. I use them on myself often, almost always in jest or in moments of truth. I use them amongst other alcoholics for jocular identification. But for many of us, even the word "alcoholic" carries something greater and deeper than just the fact that we cannot ingest alcohol in any normal manner.

I recall a time standing in front of my mirror, years before going to treatment, mouthing the words, "I'm an alcoholic." I couldn't say it out loud. While I was cognizant of what I truly was, announcing who and what I truly was, even to myself, surrounded me with some shame.

To an active alcoholic, wearing shame is as common as a dog wearing a collar and leash. It tends to direct us, move us, and place us in a spot where only more drinking can cover up the terrorizing triumvirate of shame, guilt and remorse. This further drinking then brings us deeper into the shame. Lather, rinse and repeat.

The stigma of being an alcoholic or even an addict is something I understand. I get it. I see others in and out of the rooms who struggle with "the 'A' word." Attaching themselves to that word is almost like buying into the distorted and uninformed societal view of who and what we are. The morally maligned. The weak of willpower. Emotionally bereft hedonists. Street sweepers who shotgun men's cologne underneath a bridge in a cardboard box.

We clearly are not those things, although circumstances may bring us to physical, mental and emotional pitfalls. And yet, with all the information out there about alcoholism and addiction readily available, we are still in many ways that kid in the class who eats worms: no one understands why he does it, nor wants to, and the others do everything possible to avoid him. We are the ones whispered about in the hallways scattered about in our lives.

What held me back from recovery many years ago wasn't the acknowledgment of my condition, but the idea that others would know, that the truth would be unearthed, that my secret would no longer be. That I would be stamped with an "A" and forever be identified as weak and undisciplined. That I would be drafted a failure, that no one would look at me in the same light, that the whole hollow world I had created would crumble at the touch, and that all eyes would peer at me in disgust.

I knew what others thought of alcoholics and addicts; I too had those very same thoughts. I didn't want to be one of them — and that's what stopped me in my tracks, even when I knew that my alcoholism was progressing quickly. Although I knew that treatment and recovery were what I needed, what I desired, my pride and ego held sway. How I thought I would be branded kept me in the muck and mire of my mess.

The stigma I felt towards myself and what others would perhaps think of me was also based on the thought that I was terminally unique — completely different than my fellows. Maybe I wasn't normal, but I wasn't one of those alcoholics. What I saw in recovery, being in the rooms of AA and surrounded by other alcoholics and addicts, was that I was not alone. I saw men and women who were like me, who drank like me, who felt like me. Our external circumstances were varied, but deep down, we were linked by something that transcended all that.

The Gift of Self-esteem

Lisa N.

Not surprisingly, my self-esteem was at an all-time low when I entered recovery. I had not accomplished anything of great promise. I could not stick with commitments to myself or others. I felt shameful, ugly, stupid, lost and spiritually void. If you had asked me, "Who Is Lisa N.?" I would have answered, "She is a miserable alcoholic failure." I knew that I needed to make a substantial change in order to pull myself from the mire of self-hatred.

I had no idea how to change, so I asked for help in AA. That plea for help was my first real act of self-love. By taking that one action, my esteem has blossomed in spurts and starts over the years. Joining AA was the first commitment I have ever made *and* kept. The discipline I have gained has helped me not just to stay sober, but also to feel a healthy sense of pride (a.k.a. "esteem") that comes from being consistent.

I've learned that action *must* accompany any attempt at a shift in thinking, such as transforming self-hatred into self-love. I can look in the mirror today and say, "I love myself. I am worthy. I am beautiful." Yet, if I continue with behaviours that nullify these affirmations, nothing is gained. If I lie, cheat, steal, and fail to meet my commitments, I am plagued by guilt and remorse — the very bandits of self-esteem.

All the mantras in the world are useless if I don't start practicing new behaviours. To learn new behaviours, I had to do some things that did not come naturally (like the Twelve Steps!), but which resulted in laying a solid foundation upon which my esteem could be built.

Coming out of great isolation and developing relationships with others were essential steps toward self-love and discovering who I really was. I believe relationships are the mirrors of ourselves. My sponsor was the first person with whom I could safely embark into such unknown territory. She provided me with an example of how to give and receive love. She loved me until I could love myself. Of course, her love was not enough in itself; I had to venture out and start to foster other relationships. Without my sponsor's mentorship, though, the journey would have been impossible.

Friendships have provided me with such an abundance of love, it often brings tears to my eyes. Today, I have the truest of friends. We count on each other. Flaws and all, we love each other and we love ourselves more as a result.

For years in AA, I sought esteem externally. Self-seeking pervaded my actions. If I was a perfect little "Miss AA" and I did all the things you told me to do, then you would like me and accept me. If I had a respectable job, I was valuable. If I had a nice home I could be proud of, I was okay. If people spoke well of me, I was at ease.

Although faulty in motive, these means did help me develop self-worth to some degree; however, I have since discovered they do not define who I am. Moreover, they do not make me "loveable." I must love myself regardless of whether you like me or not; I must love myself even if I am not set in my career; I must love myself even if I do not have all the material things I think I should have at this stage of my life. If I constantly focus on emotional dependencies and externals to make me happy, I will end up lonely and depressed.

I have had to become comfortable with my humanness and embrace my imperfections. Letting go of judgment toward myself and others was essential. To come to such a place, I had to develop a solid relationship with my higher power, which for me is that quiet intuitive voice that guides me to right action. This connection enables me to live with authenticity, to make good decisions in my life and to love others.

I do many things to nurture my self-esteem — some are ridiculously simple, like making my bed in the morning. Others are more difficult, like meeting deadlines and keeping commitments, helping others, or paying bills on time. I have to be gently honest with myself and others, even when honesty is not met with approval.

I do simple things that make me feel good, like reading, biking, exercising, seeing films or educating myself. I have learned to forgive myself when I am not able to do my best. Energy fluctuates and I can't be perfect all the time. Letting go of perfectionism has played an important role in this process of self-love.

Dr. Wayne Dyer made a statement that had a tremendous impact on me, "Change the way you look at things, and the things you look at change." He also said, "You all have a choice to make today: to see the world as a horrible place filled with hatred and terror; or to see the world as an abundant source of love." At eight years sober, I realized that I had been choosing to see the world as a terrible place. My skewed self-image was a result of this vision.

I decided to make a commitment to therapy so that I could change the way I saw things. My self-esteem has improved dramatically. My therapist has taught me how to change the way I think on a cognitive level. She questions when I say "I can't" and asks me to consider the possibility of "I can." I no longer berate myself to convey a false sense of modesty to others, because she has shown me how my language has the power to shape my thinking. The lessons continue.

Every day I take action and choose to see the universe as a benevolent system, intricately weaving its beautiful fabric. I love myself and everyone else in a way I never thought possible. What a gift!

Shame and Guilt Affect Family Members, Too

Rick J.

I grew up in alcoholism. I have chosen three alcoholic partners. I have been affected by the alcoholism in the people I love and have loved. I have my own disease. It is called Alcoholism — The Family Disease.

This disease has manifested itself in my life in a myriad of ways: I picked people who needed me; I had an overwhelming and seemingly insatiable appetite for approval; I readily adopted the victim and/or martyr role; I had an intense desire to be close to others, yet I would do everything I could to push other people away; and I have been haunted by a deep-seated sense of shame and an all-encompassing feeling of guilt.

No one ever said I was dumb, stupid or worthless. I just felt that way. Everything I ever tried, in any of the many alcoholic situations I found myself in, failed.

I felt either that I hadn't done enough and if I had done only a bit more I could have gotten the change I wanted, or that I'd done everything I could have and wondered, "Why is nothing changing?" I tried everything I could, and nothing worked.

As a child and teenager, I was embarrassed by the antics of both of my parents, alcoholic and non-alcoholic. They were the ones making fools of themselves. I couldn't show my face.

A stark memory of childhood is an occasion where my mother, terrified of what would happen when my father came home, packed a suitcase and dragged me and my sister to the home of a friend, so that we could escape yet another night of alcoholic terror. We had no car, so as the three of us ran down the street, suitcase in hand, to catch a bus, all of the kids on our street began calling out "where are you going, where are you going?" I wanted to disappear. How could I say we were running away from my Dad? I felt so worthless, so different and so inadequate.

I developed this sense of total secrecy about everything. I shared nothing, told nothing and did my best to show no feeling. I became an actor. I hid behind whatever role I judged was needed in any given situation. Who I was, clearly, was not good enough, so I adopted the characteristics of those I was with, or the situation I was in, in order to feel like I fit. It gave me a temporary sensation of fitting in, but in the end, it just compounded my feeling of being "a wrong."

This went on into my adult life and into three failed relationships with alcoholic women. The shame around those relationships ... wow! Growing up the way I did, only to find myself repeatedly choosing alcoholic women, really sent me for a nosedive. It was at the end of the third relationship that I started to get serious about my recovery. The guilt and shame were intense.

I heard definitions of guilt and shame early on that have stuck with me to this very day. Guilt is, "I have done something wrong." Shame is, "I am a wrong." I identified with both of them.

For as long as I can remember, I had felt guilty about other people's actions. I believed that it was something I had done, or didn't do, that caused their behaviour. In recovery, I learned that I don't have that kind of power. I was told that I didn't cause the alcoholism, that I can't control the alcoholism and that I certainly cannot cure it.

What I can do, however, is work on my own recovery to overcome those things that haunt me. I was told that sometimes I feel guilty because I am guilty. I did and said some very nasty things in the situations I was in. I was an equal and willing participant. If I was to overcome my feelings of guilt for things that I had done, I needed to clean up my side of the street. I have made the amends for the wrongs I inflicted on others and my feelings of guilt have been greatly reduced.

A saying I use often today in relation to the actions of others is, "Does it have my name on it?" If it doesn't (which is most of the time), I do not have to do anything about it. How absolutely freeing that is!

It gives me the space to live my life and not be burdened by the lives of others. Being responsible for my own life is a full-time job. I don't need to be responsible for anyone else's.

Shame was, and still can be, a big snag for me. On some level, I still deal with the erroneous belief that I am "a wrong." It is not at the same level it used to be, but it remains an ongoing and vital piece of my personal recovery and growth.

The Al-Anon fellowship and the Twelve Steps of AA have provided the way out for me. Alcoholism is a disease. The alcoholics in my life are not bad people. They are just alcoholics.

I am not a bad person either. I am just someone who was affected by a disease (not by a person) and then afflicted with his own disease — the family disease of alcoholism. They are recovering from their illnesses and I am recovering from mine.

My guilt and shame have not been diminished because the people I love have stopped drinking, but because I accepted the fact that I needed help and have taken the necessary actions in recovery to get that help.

A New Freedom

Carolyn G.

I'm an alcoholic and an addict and my name is Carolyn. By God's grace and the freedom the Twelve Steps have given me, it has not been necessary for me to take a drink or a drug for over a decade. I take a spiritual treatment and live a life guided by spiritual principles instead. Let me explain how a statement, so often heard, applies to me personally:

I drank for more than 20 years. I found the release from care, boredom and worry that I so identify with described in the chapter, *"A Vision for You"* in the Big Book of Alcoholics Anonymous. Why?

In *"The Doctor's Opinion"* at the beginning of the Big Book, the statement is made that "Men and women drink essentially because they like the effect produced by alcohol." I know I drank for the effect of drunkenness, but for years, I never really investigated what that meant for me. I now know the effect I was seeking was courage and freedom from care.

To me, booze was a cup of courage or a cup of "I don't care." I was paralyzed with fear of people, fear of judgment, fear of failure, and the certainty that everyone would reject me if they knew how useless, afraid and empty I was. So I had to drink to get the courage to connect with my fellows and to forget about me. I had to drink to stop caring about what you thought, what was right, what was wrong. I had to drink for freedom from the bondage of self.

The self-centredness that is the root of my alcoholism compels me to always think of me. Me, me, me, me, me, me, me ... ! I can't help it. I did what I wanted with little or no care for how it would affect others. My wonderfully loving family (as I have since come to know them) suffered greatly for fear that I would die a miserable, lonely, alcoholic death and they would have to sweep up the pieces.

I didn't care. Freedom from care was so sweeping with me it never even occurred to me what pain I might be causing to others, let alone me — except when I'd emerge sober at the end of a binge. The hideous Four Horsemen of Terror, Bewilderment, Frustration and Despair described the prison of my mind.

Eventually, my alcoholism progressed to the point where freedom was unachievable except through oblivion. The best I could hope to achieve was to blackout or pass out. My mind constantly nattered, You're useless, what a loser, no one loves you, today is the day they will discover you are a fraud and then you will have to kill yourself ... but you're so weak you can't even do that, so you'll have to live in constant terror. These thoughts were inevitably supplanted by, Those bastards, it's all their fault, I had to do what I did to survive, I'm cursed or possessed ... that's the problem. My thoughts began to be dominated by the remorse for the consequences of living a conscienceless life.

I wrestled endlessly between those two polarities: better than/less than. Somewhere I crossed an invisible line, where I was never again able to achieve that freedom of feeling a part of the human race — an equal among my fellows. My solution (alcohol) had become my problem. It had given me what I needed for so many years that I refused to admit it wasn't working anymore — until I hit my bottom.

Why is it I hit my bottom then? I don't know. I have no reasonable explanation for my shift from chasing the long-lost solution to finally giving up and saying, "I can't do this anymore. I need help. I can't drink or use anymore." I can only credit my new-found sanity to an act of providence.

Why is it that I finally stopped wrestling with the obsession that I could again experience the freedom from my poisonous mind if only I could drink enough or find the right combination of drugs, booze and behaviour? Was it luck, coincidence, accident? Or was it God? All I know is that one day I was fighting to get out and always failing, and the next day I surrendered. Surrender means we don't have to fight any more. To cease fighting anyone or anything is real freedom.

So it was through my surrender that I was able to finally hear a true message of hope in my hopelessness. I went to 12-step meetings, got a sponsor who had had a spiritual awakening as the result of the

Steps, and took the directions in the Big Book to hopefully acquire the same. I had only a speck of belief that it would work for me. Mostly, I just believed that it had worked for them.

So I dove deeply into the Steps with all that I had, which wasn't much because I was completely beaten. I saw clearly that I was held hostage by my own sick thinking and that there had to be a change if I was to live happily. The fear of drinking and the realization of the need for change gave me sufficient willingness to do whatever was necessary to achieve freedom. My spiritual experiences along the way gave me the courage to do the work.

"A Vision for You" promises that we will again find the release from care, worry and boredom in the fellowship of AA, that our imaginations will be fired and that we will make lifelong friends. That has been my experience. I am so happily sober. With this happy sobriety, I have had the freedom to pursue my dreams. The Ninth Step promises that we will find a *new freedom*. I understand from my own experience that this is the freedom from the bondage of self.

If any of you feel trapped by the compulsion to drink and think, I promise you that freedom from that madness and sadness is possible. To be free enough to spontaneously act in the genuine best interests of others and to witness love in action is a freedom that sings to the universe, "Thank you for keeping me alive long enough to feel this moment."

Thank you for my sobriety.

The Detective's Gift

Alex H. (Punanai 2003)

June 6, 2002 was a landmark day in my life. Though not my sobriety date, the day is special to me because it marks the beginning of my awareness of this gift called recovery, which was given to me in a rather unconventional way by some of Toronto's Finest from the Major Crimes Division.

As a using drug addict and alcoholic, the police were always seen as the enemy — people to be wary of, to look over my shoulder for, and to avoid at all costs. It had never crossed my mind that they could actually be the people that jump-started me on my path towards recovery, but they were.

For a five-year period in my teens and early twenties, I loved cocaine and alcohol more than I loved anything. The two substances trumped everything in my life in terms of their importance. With their help, I did seemingly irreversible amounts of damage to my family, professional, personal and psychological lives.

In the height of my addiction, I was a well-paid, high-achieving employee at a large company, and decided they weren't paying me enough to sustain my lifestyle. One of the "benefits" of my job was that I was solely responsible for a safe full of money, which ultimately became my personal drug money account after I devised what I thought would be an untraceable way of stealing from it.

It was a hot Tuesday evening, that particular June 6. I had been under investigation by the police for allegations of fraud, theft and public mischief. In my conversations and interrogations with the police, I had spun an impossible-to-maintain web of lies, and it all came crashing down on me at my mom's dinner table that night.

The process of being arrested was traumatizing to me, and the police were angry with me, to say the least. My mother was frantic, screaming at me and asking me why they were arresting me. The best I could do while being handcuffed at her dinner table was to say, "I don't know, Mom, I don't know." The statement made by the arresting detective in the following moment was to change the way I looked at myself in a profound way, because with one simple, pointed observation, he totally shattered my ego.

He said, "Look at you Alex, look at how sick you are — you're 23 years old, being arrested for a crime we know you committed, and you're not even enough of a man in your own mother's house to tell her what you did." What he said to me hurt me so much I couldn't even make sense of it at first. But then I saw myself, standing there in my mom's living room, handcuffed, arrested, being dishonest right until the bitter end, and it dawned on me that something had to change. Eventually, everything changed.

As the result of my arrest for the crimes I committed, my family checked me into treatment in July, 2002. I went there because I wanted to avoid jail time, but there was also an increasingly large part of me that was aware that I had to change the way I was living, which was most likely going to include stopping the alcohol and cocaine. While in treatment, I was taught some very useful tools that would eventually help me when it became time for me to truly seek out recovery.

I finished treatment and came back home, but didn't apply what I had learned, and relapsed almost immediately. I remember the counsellors in the treatment centre saying that if I did relapse, my using would be ruined because I would have "A head full of AA and a belly full of beer." Were they ever right!

The first time I drank and used, I had those counsellors' warnings flying around my head, but I also found that something else quite peculiar had remained in my mind: it was that statement the arresting officer had made to me a few months back, accompanied by the images of the horror my mother was forced to endure as the result of my using.

I was a stubborn addict, and kept using for another year. On some of my darkest nights while under the influence, I would say to myself repeatedly, "You're not even enough of a man to be honest with your own mother." In September of 2003, I couldn't take it anymore and decided to reach out for help again.

Today, I am approaching 10 years sober with the help of two great treatment centres, Alcoholics Anonymous, three great sponsors, a supportive family and amazing friends. I truly believe my path would have been different if I had not been arrested that night in June 2002, and I am grateful to the police, and to that one officer in particular, because without his words on one of the worst days of my life, I wouldn't have been able to see myself for who I really was.

Throughout the course of my recovery, I have made a number of amends, and one of them was to the arresting officer in my case. One day, while walking past the 52 Division in Toronto, it dawned on me that I needed to thank him for what he had done for me. I was informed that he no longer worked there, but was given his contact information at his new division.

I summoned the courage to phone him, and was grateful when he didn't answer, but left him a shaky-voiced message anyway. That night, I was standing in the parking lot after my home group ended, and a call came in from a number I didn't recognize — it was him.

I asked him if he remembered me, and he said he did. I told him that I was phoning him to thank him for the professionalism he treated me with during my arrest, and repeated to him the statement he made to me back in 2002, informing him that it was perhaps the major catalyst in me eventually being able to get sober and get into recovery.

He sounded a bit speechless, and then he said, "Thank you for making this call to me. I have been on this job for 10 years now, and have never had this experience. I am honestly stunned. Thank you. You have my phone number now, and if you ever need anything, you call me."

We wished each other well, and I have never seen or spoken to him again, but have kept him in my thoughts and prayers and am forever grateful for his fleeting presence in my life.

Sobriety 102

Sylvia H. (Walker 1995)

My name is Sylvia and I am an alcoholic.

I wrote about my sobriety for TGIF over nine years ago. And now I am going to write to you about how I lost my sobriety after I celebrated 18 years.

I went to Renascent in April of 1995. It was the best decision of my life to get clean and sober and finally get the help I needed. I had no problem admitting that I was an alcoholic and drug addict, so half the battle was won. The hard part was the other half of the battle — keeping my sobriety!

And I did pretty well for 18 years. I did what was I was told to do: I got a sponsor, I joined a group, I got active and I started working the Steps. I was feeling good; staying clean and sober. My life was getting better and better. I was employable. I stopped working in the clubs, and I had my family and friends back in my life. At nine years of sobriety, I got married and had a child.

I went through periods of my sobriety where I was a Stand-Up Alcoholic and went to my meetings, to AA retreats and Big Book studies too, and then there were times where I would be totally off the beam and not go to meetings. It's funny how easy it is for me to think I can take the wheel, go it alone, do this life without my Higher Power and leave it to my own devices! Bad thinking on my part.

Just before my 18-year mark, I separated from my husband. My eight-year-old daughter was having a hard time with our new life and the separation of her parents. I was not attending meetings, did not have a sponsor, nor was I asking God to help me and direct me. I was just a ticking time bomb waiting to explode, and I didn't even know it!

And then came the day when I took my first sip of alcohol over at my folks' place, nervous before going out on a date. Just one swig, that's all I took, but I took it.

Then, a few of my old fears came back to visit, and the only way I could handle them was to drink — because I had cut myself off from all the supports of my sobriety. And lo and behold, before I knew it, I was drinking a beer at lunch with the girls from work. Now, most of them knew I didn't drink, but I did it anyway. And they would say to me, "See, you don't have an alcohol problem — you can control it!" Ha, if they only knew.

I started to date a lot. I would not tell the guys that I was an alcoholic, and I started drinking with them. No one knew that I would wake up three hours later feeling horrible, feeling guilty and cradling myself like a baby, because I couldn't believe that I drank. So that went on for over one and a half years until my last drink. Let me share the story with you.

I went to Cuba with my daughter, now 10 years old, and I knew that I was going to drink. I got drunk the first day we were there. After my sister-in-law and my daughter noticed the change in my demeanour, they smelled the drink and said, "Hey, this has alcohol in it!" I pretended that I didn't know, that I thought it was a non-alcoholic pina colada. What a deceptive person I had become. I would go and get beers for the friends I made down there, and I would swing to the bar, down three beers and then come back with a non-alcoholic beverage for myself.

It was finally enough. I stopped and had my last drink on July 3, 2014.

When I came back home to Toronto, I got back in touch with my sponsor. I told him everything, and as fabulous as he always is, he still accepted me with open arms. He told me what I had to do, which was be honest, share, go to meetings, get active and work the Steps in my life. And don't drink!

I've had to do a lot of soul searching and working through issues that I had never dealt with, even in my 18 years of sobriety. It brought me to my knees, and I am still working through it. The guilt of going back out. The shame of telling my dear friends in AA that I went back out. It was really, really difficult. But I had to be honest and share and let people know that no matter how long you are sober, you are still only one arm's length from that first drink.

I have shared at meetings about my going back out. There is still some sense of shame, and I am still upset with myself. But I have learned that no one can take away my 18 years, and also that my sobriety is a Daily Reprieve. I do not count the days like I did when I was first sober. I have to live in today, and I can't take back yesterday, but I can live in today, one day at a time. I want to enjoy the journey, no matter how difficult it is.

All I can say to you who are reading my story is never get cocky or think your time in the program will keep you safe, because it won't. I am living proof of that. Don't do what I did. Cherish your sobriety, no matter what you are going through. Reach out to people who will lift you and help you along your journey. Don't go it alone as I did. Guard your sobriety with your all your Heart, Soul and Mind.

Wishing you much love, peace and happiness in your continuing sobriety.

It's a Good Day to be Sober

Wayne D. (Sullivan 2001)

If I have learned anything in this program, it is that there are no coincidences involved in what happens during my day. The fact that I don't manage my day anymore makes it very important that I maintain a constant vigilance for what it is that Harrold (the God of my understanding) has in store for me.

It seems that He feels that I have managed quite well in learning how to stay sober. There haven't been any lessons in this area that I have noticed for quite a while now. He has been a pesky little devil, though, when it has come to setting up lessons for me in the art of living sober each day.

For the longest time, I wasn't aware of what Harrold was up to. Everything wasn't great each and every day, as I thought it might be in AA. Things went wrong and it was up to me to do the legwork to deal with these situations.

I started out by making coffee and setting up for meetings at my home group, The Golden Mile. I went (and still go) to its Business Meetings. I was its Librarian, General Service Representative (GSR) and Intergroup Representative. This was all Harrold's way of teaching me how to place "Principles before Personalities."

When I was the GSR, didn't Harrold go and give me cancer. You dirty little bugger, I thought. (He is the God of *my* understanding and is therefore used to me talking like this.)

He gives better than He gets, though. In discussions with Him on the topic of "How to Beat Cancer," He felt that it was best to let the doctors think they were in charge of things, and that I just needed to be where He put me and do what I was told. He took care of the doctors, too (though they hardly even noticed Him). They seemed to think my attitude toward the disease was more uplifting than other patients they dealt with.

After He helped me to beat the cancer, He sent me back to my GSR position to resume my service obligations. Well, in my absence, they'd given some of my duties to someone else, so I left the position. "You'll be our Intergroup Rep, then," said my group. "Okay," I said. Now He has seen fit to give me a little job with the GTA Intergroup at 234 Eglinton, where AA business is done for all the groups in the GTA.

My experience with "Principles before Personalities" has come in handy with the work I do at our Intergroup office, where other trusted servants sometimes get these two mixed up. Along the way, He has even allowed me to cultivate a number of good friendships. I could not have done this! How is it that this is happening to me today?

You will find out, no doubt, that Harrold has a sense of humour about him. For me, this was evidenced in the Twelfth Step. This is where He said to me, "Go ahead, I can't wait to see what we can do with you practicing these principles in all your affairs." It is here that I find today's biggest and most important lessons, and it is here that Harrold allows me to use all of the Twelve Steps to live a happy, sober life day by day.

Yes, I have been given a glimpse of hope, but Harrold's light has shown me that life isn't always going to be the way I want it. And Alcoholics Anonymous has taught me that I can't do anything the way I did it before I got sober. It has meant a lot of changes — to me, by me and for me.

Our book, *Alcoholics Anonymous*, has given me the directions to follow and my new-found friend, Harrold, has given me the guidance and direction I have prayed for every day. He is working on my selfishness and self-centredness that I pray every day to have removed.

Today, Harrold has me somewhat worried. We have just finished reading in my group's Big Book discussion meeting that I "should not hesitate to visit the most sordid spot on earth on such an errand" and "keep on the firing line of life with these motives and God will keep [me] unharmed."

This has stuck with me. Because of the fact that there are no coincidences in this program, I am presently trying to upgrade my methods of being constantly vigilant while I am trudging along my road to a happy destiny.

May you all be Joyous and Free.

We Have Our Daughter Back

Liz S. (Family Program)

My journey to recovery began with anguish and hopelessness. My beloved child was sinking deeper and deeper into life-threatening addiction. I didn't know where to turn. I was hoping for an instant solution to all the heartaches and frustrations that come with loving an alcoholic. It was not to be that easy. This was a family issue, with my daughter's siblings also gravely concerned, because it was clearly evident that we were in a battle against time.

Were we worried sick? Yes! Were we feeling hopeless and frustrated? You bet! We did not understand addiction and how the substance consumes the addict. Why couldn't she just quit? Little did we know of the anguish and self-hatred that she felt every minute of every day.

By the grace of God, my son, who had been doing some research, gave me the number to Renascent. That phone call was the first step in the journey to recovery for my daughter and me.

After a three-week 12-step program at Renascent and 15 weeks of aftercare with dedicated addiction counsellors, my daughter is healthy, happy and working in a profession where she understands, and can share her experience with, others who are struggling with addiction, often compounded with mental health issues.

She has her life back and we have our daughter, sibling and beloved Auntie back, who was lost to us for almost 30 years. It was the grace of our Higher Power who put all these wonderful people in place to help her with her recovery.

My own recovery began at the same time when I took the Family Care course at Renascent. I began to understand how addiction takes over and wreaks such terrible havoc on the addict and her/his family. It's out to destroy us, but there is help. Knowledge is power; it takes hard work and dedication, not to mention humility, to recover.

A counsellor said to me, "There is a chair with your name on it at Al-Anon," and I have been going ever since. It truly is a wonderful fellowship of relatives and friends of alcoholics who share their experience, strength and hope in order to solve their common problems. We believe that alcoholism is a family illness and that changed attitudes can aid recovery. Al-Anon has but one purpose — to help families of alcoholics. We do this by practicing the Twelve Steps, by welcoming and giving comfort to families of newcomers, and by giving understanding and encouragement to the alcoholic.

It is never too late to begin again. I am so grateful for this 12-step program that is teaching me to live one day at a time.

Now What?

Paul S. (Punanai 2011)

John is a good friend of mine. He's a shining example of recovery, and I have been blessed to have him in my path and as an ally. I turn to him for his advice about recovery and, more specifically, about my own journey. He's a gentle soul with a biting tongue and measured responses.

He has known me for awhile now, so he is aware of how fastidious I can be at times. I will call him, often in a calm panic, about things that I already know, but need confirmation about. It's almost like he's the green light I need. He's the tarmac marshal on the ground, guiding the plane the last 20 feet into the terminal, light sticks and all. I go to him (and a few select, oh so lucky, others) to make sure my T's are crossed properly. He's the Reverend Lovejoy to my Ned Flanders.

John mentioned to me awhile ago that I was "scrupulous." I knew it wasn't a compliment, exactly, but I also knew that he said it out of love and concern. It's been months since he said that and it's been in my head churning slowly like freshly made bratwurst. I was offended and confused at first, but then realized it would be better if I actually looked up the word before planning my next outrage. To wit:

> *Scrupulous:*
> *1. (of a person or process) Diligent, thorough, and extremely attentive to details.*
> *2. Very concerned to avoid doing wrong.*

So although I am down with the first one, I was a little taken aback by the second. While they both seem very similar, there are some marked differences. The first definition is positive, while the second has a negative connotation. Guess which one John was connecting me to?

You see, the reason I bristled at this "scrupulous" tag was that I didn't see myself that way. Surprise, surprise — I get annoyed when someone sees something in me that I think I'm not. Especially when it's not positive. So, after brushing off the dust of my own incredulity, I started to allow this to absorb. I let it sink to where it needed to sink. And it brought up lots of things for me.

The one thing I have learned in recovery is that people aren't perfect. I know, crazy proposition, eh? I reckon that I was always trying to be Mr. Perfect in my active days. I certainly made a habit of trying to perfect the slow death I had embarked upon in my drinking. In school, I strove for 100%. I sometimes got it; other times wished I had gotten it. Nothing in between. All-or-nothing stuff. Perfectionism. What a crippling hatchet. But bred in the bone.

So, now sober, and knowing that I cannot ever achieve perfection, I began to open myself up to being wrong. I almost liked being wrong — it was one more thing to fix. Another opportunity to take a Universal Mulligan and start again. Learn from the errors. Tally up yet another failure and move on. I had convinced myself that I had no issues with making mistakes, messing up, tripping over my own inadequacies and seeing myself for the flawed yokel that I was.

Poppycock.

What I have come to realize is that I am still afraid to make mistakes. I harbour no ill will in admitting my wrongs; I am good at that. I concede my errors, make the apology and move on, resentment-free. But I still do not like making mistakes. It's that all-or-nothing thinking again, wrapping me up in an unrealistic view of life.

Why is there this need for me to not make errors, even in recovery? I know in my mind that it's going to happen, something to be embraced almost, nothing to be ashamed of. It's just taken a long time for it to hit my heart. To scrape off the old wallpaper of perfectionism and brush on this imperfect pattern of acceptance and humility and selflessness. Cull a few nasty branches off the Ego Tree. And take a few good whacks at the trunk while I'm at it. I am starting to actually embrace this through actions rather than sanctimonious intellectualizations.

So I have quietly, organically, without plan, begun an effort to follow every mistake or lack of judgment or error with a "Now what?" Okay, so I screwed up by double-booking job interviews. Now what? I called one of the candidates back and he cheerfully took a new time. Done. So I made a mistake in not doing something I promised my wife. Now what? Do it. Stop overthinking it. Done.

"Now what?" allows me to be gentle on myself — with the added bonus of prompting me to take action. Two powerful words. I don't feel the need to hammer myself so much when I mess up. I can look around and see that I am human, that this imperfection is what makes us all perfect in the way we were meant to be — in an imperfect way. Without mistakes, I am not given the chance to change or grow. And that is why I love recovery — I am not only encouraged to be okay with mistakes, but I am given the tools to work with them. And to be gentle on myself. I need that these days.

~

"John, I just don't want to screw up the one thing that has given me life again," I said the other day in a crowded cafe.

"You haven't screwed up, Paul. You're here. But you're putting expectations on yourself that no one can live up to," John replied, slurping the last of his iced tea, ice cubes dancing around the glass.

"I know that ... I just fear that I will continue to mess up."

"You will. And that's okay. There isn't much difference between us and the saints," he said.

"What's that difference? That they're perfect or something?"

"Not at all. Saints are sinners that got smart. We get smarter, more open, more loving, more available. We don't become saints, but we do get closer to God."

I wiped a sudden tear away. I just wanted to know it was going to be okay. I felt that it would.

The New Normal

Kathryn E.

If someone told me 10 years ago that I was going to be a mom, I would have laughed in that person's face. As much as I love children, I never longed to take on any maternal responsibility or have little rug rats as part of my goal to dodge conventional reality. I wanted to remain a free agent, like in baseball. Keep my options open.

After all, we addicts and alcoholics are quintessential escape artists at heart. It's part of our illness, this relentless need to live "two feet above reality." I guess you can say that we suffer from what is clinically known as the "Peter Pan Syndrome." It is marked by our resolute commitment to never grow up, to never want the party to end. Instead, we simply break free from the norm and fly, fly away to that infamous address in the sky: second star to the right, and straight on till morning.

A chemically induced Neverland fly-away experience is exactly the destination I chose to travel on as a young, impressionable girl. If I'm really honest with myself, I think what I craved back then was a slice of heaven. But praying for it proved far too slow. However, unbeknownst to me, I was destined to enter a treatment centre for alcohol and drug addiction at the ripe old age of 19. Not a chance! I thought to myself. I was in my substance abuse prime or what society would call my "rite of passage" phase.

That blowout period of chaotic bliss was marked by constant highs and lows, benders and blackouts followed by the recyclable three R's: remorse, remission and relapse. I had no plan to quit or slow down my consumption. That is, until I was forced into a residential treatment program through the Addictions Foundation in Winnipeg by my parents — a strategic move on their part. Checkmate.

Fast forward my life to the present. Who would have thought that I would be working in the addiction and mental health field as a professional support group facilitator for people living with concurrent disorders? God sure does have a sense of humour. More importantly, He has a plan and a purpose for my life: a plan that involves living for more than just me or my cravings — the care of my precious seven-year-old son.

One thing parenting in recovery has taught me is that it is a gift, and that like a garden, it needs consistent tending. Recovery is a kind of tightrope walk, which means that I need to approach the way I parent the same way I do my sobriety — with care and caution. If I don't pay attention to how I live my life, and forget to make a conscious daily effort to implement clean and sober principles and practices, I will lose my balance and take a tragic tumble off the tightrope. Of course, recovery is not an exact science. But neither is parenting. So I just do the best I can with the resources I've been given.

I try not to forecast too much into the future these days with my own worrisome brand of "what if" scenarios regarding my own adopted son's prenatal history. Given his genetic predisposition to addiction as well, I sometimes fret over whether he too will be able to steer clear of the pitfalls of the so-called "party world" or cave into that insidious, superficial lifestyle.

But I have to keep reminding myself that that was then and this is now. The fact that my son is being raised in a sober, loving and stable home should count for something in terms of the environmental influence that recovery has over this pervasive family disease. So despite the hypersensitivity I have accumulated over the years being personally and professionally exposed to both heroic and horrific stories poured out by other struggling addicts/alcoholics, I no longer believe that to die addicted would be an awfully big adventure.

To me, living and parenting clean and sober — with my eyes clear and my heart wide open — is the new normal. And I like it.

My Wish for You is a Billy M.

Thomas H. (Punanai 2010)

On May 8, 2010, I walked up the stairs of Renascent's Punanai Centre to be admitted as a client for the second time. As I crossed the threshold, the scent of the place brought a flood of memories rushing into my brain. Not a good or a bad smell, just one that instantly recalled my last time completing treatment.

It dawned on me that despite my best efforts to the contrary, I had wasted seven years of my life. I had systematically destroyed any opportunities presented to me and had alienated all of the people I claimed to hold dear. In the light of day, the sobering reality (bad pun!) was that I was completely incapable of running my own life and was unable to maintain a healthy relationship with anyone.

On my second evening in treatment, the staff had to call an ambulance because I began to experience a physical detox for the first time. Shaking and vomiting in the back of ambulance on the way to Mount Sinai, I had what the literature refers to as a moment of clarity. I realized that I was going to die and that I would most likely die alone. I returned to Renascent the following morning determined to put forth the best effort that I could muster.

I was told repeatedly that it was imperative for my sobriety that I acquire a sponsor and begin to work the program of Alcoholics Anonymous to the best of my ability. My first sponsor was named Billy M.; he was and is a member of the Hill Group. He saved my life.

Billy taught me about the importance of consistency and that in order for me to stay sober I had to suit up and show up. He taught me that I needed to do service and that setting up chairs and making coffee would get me out of myself. He taught me to face my fears, by working a Fifth Step with him and sharing my past. He taught me not to confuse how I am feeling with how I am doing, that my emotions are not the truth and not to listen to my head.

These things were all vitally important but what saved me was his love. He treated me like a brother; always supportive, always encouraging and always there to help.

I have not found it necessary to pick up a drink or a drug in 1,090 days, or two years, 11 months and 24 days, at the time of this writing.

I myself am now a sponsor. I have held my guys while they wept, laughed with them at our shared ridiculousness, presented them with medallions, debated the existence of god and, in one awful case, buried one when he died after a relapse.

I believe that a sponsor is the most important relationship a person will have in sobriety and, in some cases, in life. I believe that as far back as Bill and Dr. Bob, all we have been seeking as addicts is a sense of connectivity and acceptance. My addiction wants to isolate me from the world and choke the hope from my soul. The way for me to combat this is diligent work with a sponsor and doing my absolute best to carry our message to the alcoholic who still suffers.

For some reason that eludes me, I have been given a second chance. I have been given a life that is completely unrecognizable from the one I used to live. Most days when I wake up, it takes me a second or two to realize that I'm not still dreaming.

Renascent, Alcoholics Anonymous and Billy M. saved me. Strong sponsorship with Step work brought me back to life and taught me how to live like a sober gentleman of Alcoholics Anonymous. Working with my guys today helps to keep me grounded and always puts a smile on my face.

If you are just out of treatment and struggling, my wish for you is a life like this. My wish for you is a Billy M. My wish for you is the courage to be honest and the courage to share your fears and dreams with someone else. In short, I hope you allow the power of recovery to expel the darkness inside so that you may walk in the sunshine of the spirit.

Catching Volunteer Fever

Cynthia L.

Volunteer — "A person who offers to do something for no pay."

That is the dictionary's definition of the word, but I beg to differ. My volunteer experience paid me in ways I could not even imagine.

Volunteering is exactly what I set out to do when I graduated from college in 2011. I had diplomas in Addiction Studies and Addiction Counselling and absolutely no experience of any kind. My school's Program Director suggested I call Renascent; she had worked there herself at one time. She thought I might offer my time as a volunteer.

After meeting with Renascent's House Manager, I began volunteering at the Munro Centre on Monday and Wednesday evenings from 4:00 p.m. to 8:00 p.m. when there is only one counsellor on duty and the ladies are in the house for the night. I started out by learning to answer the phone. Seems simple enough, but when you realize the impact that just saying, "Hello, Renascent, may I help you?" might have on an alcoholic or addict at the end of his or her rope, you think again. Next, I did small things like putting out the name tags for dinner, logging on the phone for overnight access, preparing a copy of the day's census for the evening counsellor to make notes with and getting the evening's video out.

I soon realized that every task I could take on would make a difference to a counsellor who just might need a minute or two to breathe — and would benefit our clients as well! Little did I know the impact it would have on me. I began feeling better about myself than I had in a long time. I had a purpose! Suddenly even making a pot of coffee was important.

Before long, I caught Renascent fever. I wanted to learn as much as I could about the organization and its programs. Where might I be of service?

I began to volunteer for the Continuing Care program as well as at Munro. This is where I saw real recovery starting to take hold of clients. Three weeks of treatment was laying the firm foundation, but here clients were learning to live life on life's terms, one day at a time. They shared their everyday struggles in the real world and how they were managing to stay sober. They were actually using coping skills taught to them in Primary Care. Of course there were relapses, but that's the reality of the disease we live with.

Within two months, I was volunteering four days a week. I was honoured to help. What had started out as a way to earn hours for certification had become a passion. I witnessed miracles every day in our clients' lives. I got to see the joy on their faces as they began to recognize that they have a Higher Power of their own. I was there to admit them on day one, when they were usually frightened or angry, or both, and I was present on graduation day when they walked out our door with their heads held high with dignity and grace.

The counsellors I have had the privilege to learn from are unwavering in this cause of battling addiction. Not once did they ever tell me they did not have time to help or answer my questions — even when they really didn't. They are truly dedicated to helping men and women recover, one person at a time, one day at a time. I believe that I learned from the best!

I no longer work as a volunteer. The counsellors did such a fine job of training me that I am now working as a full-time counsellor. What a magical ride this has been. I know that my understanding of commitment has been radically altered, my personal recovery has deepened and I am a better woman for my volunteer experience.

Bill Wilson said it best: "I was to know happiness, peace, and usefulness, in a way of life that is incredibly more wonderful as time passes."

I truly love Renascent. Thank you all.

I'm Okay ... You're Okay

Tony A.

I was first introduced to the idea of using positive affirmation when I was in a treatment centre many years ago. We were asked to repeat several one-liners like, "I'm okay ... you're okay," "I'm a valuable and lovable person," and many others.

At the time, I was quite cynical and jaded from living a horrendous life in hard-core addiction and in my mind, I could not help but to think ... you've got to be kidding me! But I am quite happy to say that today I can see the relevance of these affirmations and actually try to use them as life-affirming slogans. They have proven to have great power to influence and reprogram my thinking.

For me, the desire to incorporate these facets into my life started when I reached a point of absolute surrender to my disease, acknowledged that I could not do this on my own and turned to outside power for help. This came in all sorts of shapes and sizes that I could utilize — including using affirmations.

Now, just to be clear, I am pretty much convinced that, for me, the spiritual solution was the necessary catalyst to facilitate recovery from addiction — but I've incorporated many tools into my recovery plan and this includes using affirmative thought to support a positive mental attitude. This has become increasingly important to me over the years in my recovery.

In the morning, I meditate and have a period of quiet time and reflection. During this quiet time, I read spiritual meditations and often try using affirmations. I will say these affirmations while looking directly at myself and into my eyes as I repeat them to myself. I must admit that sometimes this feels a bit awkward but I do it anyway. Like many of the practices that I have cultivated over the years, it all began with simply just doing them regardless of how I felt. The unfamiliar eventually does become the familiar.

For me, these practices are intensely practical and have proven to be quite enlightening. I've experienced inner peace and tranquility as well as a new confidence and shift in perspective as a result of these practices. And to think I almost missed them. Remember, when I was first introduced to them, I scoffed and thought they were a bunch of nonsense and would not work for me.

Step by step and day by day, these little gems have assisted in the transformation of my thinking and my energy. I have learned to embrace and honour the loving spirit within, which is something that I had been quite afraid of, actually. Being kind, gentle and loving in all of my affairs often requires work and practice. Affirmations can assist with this.

Believing that I am enough is another area that I need to pay special attention to with the use of affirmative thought. As I have learned through many fearless and searching inventories, I have acquired the painful belief that I am not enough and this is manifested in many forms. Having been privileged to sponsor many men and women over the years and to hold the sacred trust that has formed in many of these relationships, I have learned this is a uniform truth or core belief of many of us recovering from addictions.

I have found the workplace and my family of origin to be the institutions to carry this top priority rating, as the emotional attachments that are formed remind me to pay special attention to these. For example, when I made the conscious understanding that freely giving was a big part of my experiencing joy in life, I tried to bring this concept into my workplace. A simple little attitude change has proven to bring a profound shift in how I have come to relate to my workplace and serve the organization. Again, I say that affirmations are powerful!

It is like I am rewriting the script using a more positive framework and language that eventually change my thinking and behaviour. Continuous action and vigilance are key. I also need to remind myself to be gentle with my growth, as none of this has happened quickly for me.

Through the use and practice of affirmations along with other spiritual tools, I have come to embrace, better understand and appreciate our wonderful "one day at a time" concept and this wonderful journey of recovery and healing that I have been privileged to be a part of.

Spiralling Up

Joanne S.

Alcoholism demands full participation from the family and the most insidious part of it is that you don't recall signing up. You're enlisted without your consent. The disease demands it so it can thrive.

You adjust incrementally and small changes add up. Over time, your behaviour transmutes to cope with an ever-increasingly more difficult and painful situation. You think it won't get worse but unchecked, it always does.

It wasn't easy watching someone I love commit suicide in my own home. I thought I could control the pain by fighting it. That didn't work. However, by accepting its existence, I could transcend it. And so began the process of sorting out what I could change and what I couldn't.

Through friendships with recovering alcoholics and addicts, I learned to make the distinction between the disease and the person. I had never known their befores, only their afters. Good people do bad things when they're addicted.

My anger diffused as I began to identify addiction as the supreme hijacker — a particularly clever parasite that uses every trick to ensure its host doesn't initiate divorce. It was easier to detach from my father's destructive behaviour when I understood the motivation behind it. His actions and words became less personal and powerful as I began to see them as simple mechanisms by which addiction protected its domain. An explanation certainly helped but setting limits ensured that I didn't excuse unacceptable behaviour.

Even though my father resisted recovery, I was at peace with the fact that I had done all that I could to help him. But still something kept drawing me back into the mess. I had stopped chasing after my dad, but my mom was another issue. I still gave her the power to displace me from my life and my priorities as she laboured under the weight of a partner who, over the years, lost his job, driver's license, mobility, health and periodically his mind.

I held her up and she held him up. I pulled back. She pulled back. He finally began to take responsibility for his own welfare. But he ran out of time. A body weary of years of punishment finally gave out on October 12, 2004.

My life is more simple and satisfying as principles for living well continue to click. Someone once showed me a simple image of a spiral that helped clarify how and when a family member should help an addict.

Spiralling downwards: don't touch (except, of course, for confronting your loved one with the problem and a solution). Spiralling upwards: give your full support. This image has helped both me and my mom as we deal with another close family member struggling with alcoholism. We simply ask ourselves, "Is he spiralling up?" before we invest our time and energy. But regardless, our love for him is constant either way.

Thank you, Renascent, for helping me get to this place.

A True Partnership

Roger C.

I first met Wayne in the rooms of AA.

Mind you, these were not traditional AA rooms. Wayne would have nothing to do with the "God bit" in AA and so his home group, pretty much since it was founded in the fall of 2009, was an agnostic AA group called "Beyond Belief."

I would see him there every Thursday evening in downtown Toronto. Coming directly from his job as an access counsellor at Renascent, he was always dressed up in a tie and jacket. He never told anyone that he worked at a treatment centre for alcoholics, though: he didn't want people to think that he thought he knew more about alcoholism than anyone else in the room because of where he worked.

Wayne would share at these meetings. His message was often quite simple: "Don't pick up the first drink." And he would talk about how he had failed at that himself many, many times over the years. He would deliver the message with a strange combination of grumpiness and congeniality. Maybe grumpy because it had taken him so long to heed his own message, and definitely congenial because he cared about the other alcoholics in the room and hoped they wouldn't make the same mistake.

In February of 2013, Wayne was diagnosed with lung cancer, which had spread to his hip and made it difficult for him to walk. It was at that time that I decided to try something new for me: I offered to help him out, however and whenever I could.

Both of us had isolated as alcoholics. We weren't very good at relationships and had trashed any number of them in our years as drunks. In the Big Book of AA, Bill Wilson writes: "The primary fact that we fail to recognize is our total inability to form a true partnership with another human being." Wayne and I talked about that quote. We understood it.

So over the last year of his life, I took Wayne to the hospital for CAT scans and tests and chemotherapy when they weren't being done by the Cancer Society. Sometimes we would take a cab and other times I would rent a car. I ran errands and picked up groceries for him. We talked and talked.

Most importantly for both of us, I would show up every Thursday to help Wayne get to our AA meeting. At first, I always brought him a Timmy's coffee and a cinnamon roll but eventually that graduated to a Starbucks coffee and a cinnamon brioche. I can't stand Timmy's and eventually Wayne came to prefer Starbucks. Or at least that's what he said.

He died on a Friday, March 21. Ten days earlier, I had taken him to Mount Sinai for chemotherapy and it had been downhill ever since. And he knew it. He told me that when he had first been diagnosed with cancer, he was told he had only six months to a year to live and, well, his time was up. Wayne didn't avoid any topics.

I was with him on the Thursday prior to his death. I knew he couldn't go to the meeting but I dropped in on my way to it with a Starbucks coffee and a cinnamon brioche. He couldn't talk, really. His throat was bad, and he was waiting for an IV. We hung out for an hour. We were both appalled at how much weight he had lost. The next day, we texted back and forth until the early afternoon. At around nine in the evening, I got a call and was told that he had been found dead.

Not a surprise, but still ...

I was numb for a few days. Non-functional.

But then that changed. Wayne had resolved not to die a drunk and he hadn't. And we both, to the best of my knowledge, had gotten something precious and unexpected in our recovery that had escaped us in the depths of our alcoholism.

We had over the last year of his life become friends. In spite of our inadequacies in so many other areas, we had been able to form what Bill Wilson had called a "true partnership."

These days, I am mostly grateful to have known Wayne and that he and I had been friends.

Tiny Speck, Infinite Power

Kim R. (Munro 2013)

I was reminded recently of my very early recovery days where I was either at a complete stop or speeding down the highways of sober living at 160 km/hr. My life for the last little while has been set on cruise control and so I thought that emotionally, I would be safe to re-visit the place where my journey of recovery began. I visited the Munro Centre over the Thanksgiving weekend; with this has come a lot of reflection.

I was reminded of each and every emotion that I experienced while I was there. That was very powerful. Looking back on my 21 days in treatment, my worst fears never materialized: I was not misunderstood and I was not rejected. I was understood and I was accepted. I was given the biggest gift of all: the option of either continuing to live in a state of shame or to change my innermost perceptions. The decision to choose between these two options was a gift because it put me in the driver's seat — not just in my recovery, but in my life as well. The only requirement for change was that I had to remain honest, willing and open-minded.

I was able to appreciate this gift during my visit, for I remembered the most frightening day of my recovery — my graduation day. As I watched other ladies leave the house feeling ecstatic, I was terrified. I was terrified because I had been given huge chunks of truth about myself that I knew I had to not only digest, but accept. My biggest acceptance of all was that nothing could bring me peace but myself. And that would mean tearing apart the tapestry of lies that I had so intricately weaved throughout my addiction.

I was fearful of directing my own recovery, but now I can appreciate that fear for I can understand where it came from. It came from shame, it resulted in feelings of guilt and it made me uncertain as to whether I deserved the happiness that could come from navigating life sober.

I am incredibly grateful to the counsellors for giving me the invaluable knowledge and spiritual tools that have allowed me to change my perceptions about myself and others. I do not want my old life back. I am transforming my thoughts daily into a new way of living. And that is a miracle! I have a positive foundation on which to continue my journey of healing, and that foundation is Renascent.

The faces of the ladies have changed at the house, their stories have varied to some degree, but the mission of the counsellors has remained the same. And that is beautiful. Their dedication is inspiring. Their love is reassuring. And their stories are encouraging time and time again for they remind me that change is possible.

I am a tiny speck in a huge spectrum. I never would have accepted being a "tiny speck" before, as my ego would not have allowed for such, but today I am genuinely grateful for being that tiny in such a huge spectrum. One self-seeking speck holds no power, for it is incapable of change. But many grateful specks hold infinite power, for they are capable of making change together. And this is what I needed to learn when I visited the house.

So Just ... Give Up
Martin S.

By now you know
It's not going to stop
It's not going to stop
It's not going to stop
Till you wise up

That's the refrain from Aimee Mann's haunting song "Wise Up." I first encountered those words in a powerful sequence in the film "Magnolia" which, among its several themes, addresses addiction. All the main characters, unable to endure their overwhelming personal pressures any longer, suddenly stop dead and begin singing:

It's not going to stop
It's not going to stop
It's not going to stop

This is a song about the bottom. It asks the musical question, "What now, now that all hope is gone?" Collapsed in misery, the film's characters repeat over and over the desperate chant:

It's not going to stop
It's not going to stop
It's not going to stop

Then, seemingly teetering at the edge of a dark abyss, the song ends with the phrase:

So just ... give up

In one way, that ending — just give up — could play as the ultimate, desperate defeat. Instead, it soon becomes clear that the end of the song is actually the first ray of real hope in the characters' lives, the first good intention in their long histories of bad ideas and worse results.

Just give up. Accept that it's not going to stop, whatever "it" may be.

Some time after viewing the film, I was lying half-awake in a stupor on the floor of my living room with Mann's song looping endlessly on the stereo. I finally heard the meaning behind those simple words, "It's not going to stop — so just give up," and I had my first glimmer of acceptance.

I had yet to attend my first AA meeting, yet to hear the words of the First Step or the Serenity Prayer, all of which would initiate my recovery. In the same way that I did not at first grasp the concepts of powerlessness, surrender or humility, I did not at first understand the word "acceptance." I had to patiently learn what these words meant and how they were practiced in and around AA.

But acceptance was perhaps my first act of rebellion against "the lash of alcoholism." Understanding and accepting that I had this condition — this mental obsession and physical allergy — and that in cold reality my life was in shambles, was the first groping step I took toward living in peace and sobriety.

I realized I had been fighting my hopeless dependence on drinking; fighting with everyone and everything around me. In fact, I had been fighting life. All I had to do was accept this, and make the decision to give up.

After all, what did I have to lose? The right to destroy myself and my family? The right to be overly critical and revel in anger? The right to be miserable and chilled to the bone with shame?

At first, I bemoaned what I thought of as "my lot in life." Why me? Why can't my problems just disappear? Why can't my responsibilities just vaporize and someone swoop in to take care of me? My lot in life appeared to promise nothing but endless drudgery.

But by accepting my alcoholism and its attendant spiritual emptiness, and with the acceptance of a Higher Power, I soon found that I was free to embrace life instead of fight it, and that life was good.

If all of our spiritual principles work through action, what am I going to "do" today to enact acceptance? To show surrender? To live with humility? They're fine words, but I soon lose their full implication if I don't practice them. Acting on these simple concepts can give me a powerful base for changing first my attitude toward my life and then, through the guidance of a power greater than myself, my life itself.

If I practice acceptance by working gratefully at my tasks for the day, then they're not overwhelming. If I accept my limitations and don't try to lasso the moon, then my time is manageable. If I don't try to live as a perpetual rock-and-roll monster, then I no longer have to pay for the demands of that lifestyle.

If I accept conditions as they are today, then I actually do have a fighting chance. If I humbly accept the will and objectives of a power greater than myself, who showers us with love and opportunity, then I can grow spiritually in the image of those whose examples are a beacon.

In recovery, I have sometimes had to learn the hard way to accept emotional and mental turmoil, relationship conflicts, and financial insecurities. But now, for the most part, I can accept that daily chores will accompany my daily bread, that people around me will act in mysterious ways, and that the world will spin on an axis slightly out of alignment with my reckoning. And I can accept that I will continuously make mistakes with little danger of the sky falling.

By making a choice to willingly embrace that which is placed before me, I will find that what I once bemoaned as "my lot in life" can now be accepted humbly and happily as "a lot in life" — an awful lot more than I have any reasonable right to expect.

It Was Time to Stop Waiting

Lorraine C. (Family Program)

I didn't grow up with alcoholism. I had a good childhood. My parents divorced when I was 12 and I was raised by my mother, who was very loving and nurturing. I was an independent, motivated young person.

I married a wonderful man. I knew he drank a lot but I didn't care because I liked to drink, too. We had three children whom we loved very much. We were both very dedicated parents. However, while living with active alcoholism, our family's energy was diverted from healthy emotional development to an ever-increasing focus on alcohol-related issues. Slowly, gradually, insidiously, everyone was controlled by the dis-ease.

I hadn't spent one hour of my life learning about the disease that eventually threatened to destroy everything in it. I based my life on a single piece of information about alcoholism: that people have to *want* help before anything would change. So I waited, for seven years. And every day I believed my husband when he promised that things would be different tomorrow. And they were. They were worse.

I was a passive "hostage." I became complicit in imposing overly strict expectations on the children, by allowing it to happen. This was damaging to the children, to me (especially because I knew in my heart, mind and soul that it was unhealthy) and to my spouse, because it enabled more of the same. Keeping the peace at any cost seemed to be emotionally safer at first. After a while, I was stuck in this behaviour pattern and was no longer thinking or acting according to my own heart and better judgment.

The family dynamics got to the point where everyone's emotions were dictated by the moment-to-moment mood of the alcoholic. There was often no rhyme nor reason as to why my spouse's mood would change. Today, I understand that there were always reasons, always related to alcohol.

Over time, I learned not to rock the boat because it made things even more uncomfortable than they already were. But eventually the cost of putting up and shutting up became too great. The decline in my spouse's emotional and physical health frightened me. I began quietly wondering what happened to the person I used to be. Secrecy and self-reliance kept me trapped.

"When the student is ready, the teacher will appear." The day I asked for help, a counsellor on TV explained how family secrets ensure that nobody ever talks about them. And if nobody ever talks about them, nothing ever changes.

That same day my cousin (who had gone through Renascent) came to visit. She asked how things were going and I tried to lie. Then I remembered the TV show, started to cry and told her the truth. We talked and she calmly shared what she had learned. One thing she learned is there are three outcomes for alcoholics: 1) jail; 2) insanity; 3) death. Another is that alcoholism is a progressive disease, and that my spouse would continue to get sicker, more rapidly, as time went on.

She suggested I call Al-Anon, which is for people affected by someone's drinking. I realized then that I didn't have to wait for my spouse to want help before I could get it for myself.

The Al-Anon program was a treasure find. It offered hope, education, acceptance, confidentiality, health, peace of mind, friendship and an amazing program for living. The most helpful thing I heard was other people's honesty. Their truth shattered my denial. Their emotional, physical, spiritual, economic and social health made mine attainable. I borrowed their courage until I felt my own.

I knew that facing reality was going to be very threatening to my spouse, so I kept the focus on my own experience. I was honest and quietly determined to go about the business of straightening out my life. I treated the situation matter-of-factly, as if I were dealing with a house repair. It simply had to be done.

The Renascent family worker was like a guardian angel for our family. I attended the Renascent family sessions and began to become educated about alcoholism.

My spouse saw that I was recovering my health, happiness and hope for the future. He wanted those things too, and eventually went into treatment at Renascent. He has been sober for 10 years. The Renascent Family Program, AA, Al-Anon and Alateen continue to provide each member of our family with an amazing way of living.

Today, our family has incorporated the 12-step recovery programs into our daily lives. Today, we know it's a strength to ask for help when we need it. We have an array of resources and people in recovery to guide and support us. I have the courage to think, speak and act as a separate, worthy member of the family.

It's truly amazing to have open communication with our three teenagers regarding all of the issues of substance use and recovery. We strive to allow each family member to feel safe enough to honour and express his or her own feelings, and to respect one another. We know how to recognize when we have made mistakes, and we know how to make amends and restore emotional health.

Recovery offers us countless ways to grow as individuals and as a family. It helps us to be honest and accountable to ourselves and to each other. It's been the most wonderful and exciting journey ... I'm so glad I didn't miss it.

Brand New All Over Again

Paul S. (Punanai 2011)

She found it while cleaning up.

My wife, sorting through some shelves, found our wedding photo. I hadn't seen it in many, many years. The last time I had gazed at it, it was on the floor, surrounded by broken glass and a torn frame — remnants of an argument we had one night. A night no doubt driven by, and exacerbated by, my untreated alcoholism.

My marriage was often a barometer for my own mental and emotional health. My marriage was like my drinking — on the rocks and complicated, fuelled by my ego and self-centred actions. My alcoholism had isolated me and kept me distant from the woman I had vowed to honour and cherish for the rest of our lives. I was a fading shadow — a ghost of that young man in that picture.

When I came to treatment, my wife had already asked me to leave the matrimonial home. I was living on my own for the first time in my life. We both didn't know what was going to happen, but it was clear that working on my recovery was first and foremost. Without that, everything else would crumble at the softest of breezes.

I took the advice from the old-timers who said that my Higher Power would take care of things once I took care of my recovery. I worked the Steps, kept open to new experiences, and started the process of gaining clarity and accessing what was previously shut down within. I found a connection to the Creator and found His spirit moving through and throughout me. I started to move towards healing from within so that I might heal without.

My wife needed to do her own healing as well. Living for many years beside the twister of an alcoholic husband does its own damage. It fractures and weakens. Tears and breaks. As we started to heal, we started to talk. We talked honestly and openly for the first time. Gone were the layers of deceit and resentment. We were able to come together and have real heart-felt dialogues; talks about what we wanted and where we saw ourselves. Unbeknownst to us, the process of coming together in a new and healthy way was starting to happen.

The ironic thing was that during this process, we were convinced at some level that we would not be back together. The betrayal my wife felt through my actions and secrecy took a heavy toll. The anger and hurt that my wife felt through my DUI and subsequent consequences was a burdensome cross. But somehow hope slipped through those cracks. And hope started to bloom and burst forth. Hope stemmed from my Step work and through our connection to the Creator and my wife's gradual willingness to work through our issues. I started to see that spirituality and romance could co-exist. In fact, inventory work moved me to write my romantic ideal — how I saw my wife, how I would treat her, how I would honour my commitment to her.

Fast forward a few years now and we've continued to grow in our marriage. We've had another child since. We've learned to appreciate each other in new ways. I see in her now what attracted me to her in the first place. I have learned to practice spiritual principles in my relationship with her. I have learned to see things in a new light, to practice empathy, and entertain her ideas and thoughts, rather than bulldoze through her like I used to. We have come together as a real partnership. We have never raised our voices once since we have come back together.

Our marriage is based on full honesty, devotion, patience, understanding and respect — things that I wasn't able to give way back when. We have learned to walk hand-in-hand through the rough patches and to celebrate the fun times. We've been able to come to a maturity in our marriage that we only dreamed of before everything came crumbling down.

Coming back meant doing work, and continuing to work at it. But I have come to learn that it's not just about coming back to an old marriage; it's also about creating a new one. It's a brand new marriage. And if that's the case, we're still newlyweds. And it feels like it.

My wife once told me, about a year into my recovery, something that I have never forgotten. While we were separated, she took a trip to see her friend in Florida. And while at the beach, she made a list in the sand of what she sought in a mate. Honest, spiritual, strong, open-minded, etc. And it was about six months into my recovery that she saw in me the very things she carved into the shore that day. That has shown me the power of what is possible in recovery.

That wedding picture now sits in our living room. A bit faded, a bit ragged at the edges, but there is still that bright light that shines from our eyes. Those eyes still shine bright today. But with the knowledge that we come from authentic places, and all pretence and pain dropped and washed away.

We celebrated 19 years of marriage last month. Brand new all over again.

Why Gratitude Makes Me Happy

Alida F. (Munro 2013)

> *If the only prayer you said in your whole life was 'thank you,' that would suffice.*
>
> *Meister Eckhart*

I begin each day by waking and writing three things that I am grateful for in that moment. It can be anything, and I always write down the first three things that come to my mind.

Blue skies, dew on the grass, birds singing outside my window.

Positive relationships with my friends and family, hot coffee, walking my dogs.

Soft pillows, learning to trust, a safe place to live.

This allows me to set out into the day with an attitude of gratitude and it makes me happy.

This practice was suggested to me while I was in treatment and I can remember rolling my eyes and thinking that it was a stupid idea. How could a simple act of thinking about who and what I'm grateful for make such a big difference in my life?

But then something funny happened. I took the suggestion and I started writing my gratitude list every morning. This one simple act reminds me every morning of all the positive things that I have in my life, no matter how small. There are always at least three every day.

When I was active in my addiction, gratitude was completely foreign to me and I certainly didn't appreciate any of the little things. I wanted big presents, accolades and applause. Nothing small would do. I wanted only the rewards — with none of the work.

Today, it's the smallest things that make the biggest difference. Life's little daily gifts that make me happy and grateful. I hadn't noticed them before — I wasn't aware enough to pay attention to the warm breeze or the leaves changing colour. I was fixated on what I could have, rather than what I could experience.

Adopting an attitude of gratitude helps me to see the bigger picture. If I'm stressed out at work, I can be grateful that I'm employed. If I'm upset that my bills are piling up, I can be grateful that I have a roof over my head. I can recognize that there are lessons presented to me every day — lessons that can teach me patience, acceptance and tolerance.

Being grateful also reminds me to thank others. "Thank you." Just two little words that can mean so much. Taking a minute out of my day to tell someone why I'm grateful for them is important.

People like being appreciated for who they are and what they do — it can truly make a huge difference. It costs me nothing, but makes someone else happy. And making someone else happy now makes me happy.

Before I go to bed every night I thank my higher power for my sobriety and I reflect on what I have to be thankful for that day. When I struggle to find three things that I can be thankful for — and sometimes I still struggle — I read this aloud:

I am thankful that I don't have everything I desire; if I did, there would be nothing to look forward to.

I am thankful that I don't know everything, for it gives me the opportunity to learn.

I am thankful for the difficult times, for this is when I grow.

I am thankful for my limitations; they give me opportunities for improvement.

I am thankful for each new challenge, because it will build my strength and character.

I am thankful for my mistakes; they will teach me valuable lessons.

I am thankful when I am tired and weary, because it means I've made a difference.

It is easy for me to be thankful for the good things. A life that is rich with fulfillment comes to me when I am also thankful for the setbacks.

In the Footsteps of My Father
Jack G.

Growing up in a house that was rampant with alcoholism is not that rare. But living in a house that was crazy and sick, then shifting to love and sobriety, that was a strange twist.

I didn't want anything to do with my dad when I was growing up. And I certainly did not want to be part of his sobriety.

With my mom joining Al-Anon and my dad AA, I saw how our household changed from chaos to love. Both of my parents started to shift focus as they continued to get further in their programs of recovery. The house truly started to change and these changes did not go unnoticed on my end. I witnessed the mighty shift of recovery first-hand. And this seemed to happen rapidly.

But at the time, I thought they missed the boat with me. I did not want anything to do with their programs or their new-found love for me. I was heavy into my own alcoholism and I was loving it. I was loving my booze and drugs a lot more than I was loving my family or myself.

I left my parents' house to continue on this destructive journey. But I always knew that there was another way to live — and that haunted me while hustling on the streets. Trying to drown out the truth is a sad place to be.

After being beaten down by my own addiction, knowing there was a house of love and change waiting for me started to appeal to me.

I finally collapsed with my addiction and asked for help on November 28, 2000. I've been sober and free ever since. I'm finally the man I've always wanted to be. It has taken a lot of work and changes to get my life in order, but it has been beyond worth it.

I have the most incredible connection with my family today. I am not willing to gamble a drink on what we have created. Our new lives are spectacular and I could not have what I have while fixating on drinking. I could not have what I have without Alcoholics Anonymous. Today, I am present in the moment. I don't need a substance to be real. I'm living!

My relationship with my father today is beyond words. The best way I can describe our bond — sacred. I love the word "sacred" in sobriety. Nothing was sacred before. Everything had a price and addiction had no boundaries.

Today, my relationships with God, myself and other people are sacred. And I am honoured to follow my father in his footsteps.

No Secrets, No Lies, No Excuses

Jane J.

As I sit hear pondering the topic of "What to Tell Your Children," I find myself reflecting on my own childhood. The feelings creep back as I remember an all-encompassing sense of fear; of doom and gloom; that all was not right with the world; and that I was somehow responsible.

My behaviour was directed towards trying to keep the peace and behaving in such a way that I could emotionally escape the cloud of tension and unpredictability that shrouded my environment.

Preferring solitude to company, I would spend inordinate amounts of time on my own where I could create a fantasy of what I wanted my future family life to be. There would be no yelling and no crying. I would be able to bring friends home. I would feel safe. I would tell my children every day that I loved them. My children would, I promised myself, never experience what I had experienced.

I began to drink alcoholically at the age of 16. After my first gulp, I made the decision that I would continue to drink for the rest of my life. Just a drink or two each day would be all I would need to feel happy and to function. That certainly wouldn't hurt anyone.

As my disease progressed, I continued to live in denial and was drinking alcoholically when all three of my children were conceived. I stopped during my pregnancies, believing that they would provide the time I needed to be able to control my drinking again. The elusive goal of controlled drinking!

My children, at the hands of my alcoholism, were eventually apprehended by Children's Aid. The first time was for one night; I lied my way into getting them back. The second time was for five months; I went into treatment. The third, and final, time I lost custody of them was when I tried some controlled drinking again. At this time, my oldest child was nine and my twins were three years old.

Once my children were taken for the last time, I made a wholehearted effort to drink myself to death. And several things happened, through what could only be Divine Intervention.

Obviously, even through several admissions to ICU, I survived. I knew somehow, in my deepest of hearts, in that moment of clarity, that I did not want my children to discover that their mother died an alcoholic death. I did not want them to ever feel that they had been responsible for my drinking. I wanted them to know that my disease resulted in an overwhelming compulsion to drink no matter what. I did not want them to have unanswered questions if I could at all possibly help it.

I surrendered to a power greater than myself and I sought guidance from those who had been there before me. I asked for help and I prayed.

Honesty was the only answer. No secrets. No lies. No excuses.

I sat down with my oldest child first. I attempted to explain to her that I was an alcoholic and that alcoholism is a disease. I told her that it had nothing to do with her and everything to do with me. Together, we went to see our family doctor. He explained to her the disease concept of alcoholism.

Eventually, I was allowed to take her unsupervised. I took her to meetings of AA. She met my sponsor and my AA friends. She heard other people's stories and knew that she was no longer alone.

I fought off the need to have her trust me right away and said nothing as she searched my cupboards and closets looking for booze whenever she was allowed to visit. Later, I suggested Alateen. She said she wasn't ready to go and didn't know if she ever would. I respected her decision.

My twins remain in foster care with another family. I was not given access to them as quickly as I was to my oldest child. However, I ensured, to the best of my ability, that I knew what they were being told and that it was the truth. Children's Aid told them that I was an alcoholic — that once I consumed alcohol, I lost complete control of choice. They told them that I was sick but that I was recovering.

When I was finally able to see them, I told them the same thing I told my daughter but in more simplistic terms. There was no sugar coating, no lies, no excuses, no justifications or rationalizations.

I answered their questions to the best of my ability. I did not make promises I could not keep and kept the promises that I made. When I said I'd call, I called. When I said I would visit, I visited. They, too, met my sponsor and were told that my sponsor had the same disease.

As my children grow and change and develop more questions, and as I continue to work on my recovery, I keep the lines of communication open. My visits are still arranged on a schedule that involves monthly, unsupervised access with my twins and access at my oldest daughter's discretion.

My oldest daughter no longer searches my cupboards and closets and makes no attempt to smell my breath. She is, by her own admission, still angry and hurt. However, I have told her that support is available to her whenever she is ready. She still does not wish to go to Alateen. That is up to her.

I am well aware that children of alcoholic parents are at a higher risk of developing a substance abuse problem themselves. I used to worry myself sick about that. I still catch myself worrying. When I do, I remember *Yesterday, Today and Tomorrow*, and stay in the day.

I am grateful to be alive, to have regular visits with my children, to hear their voices, to feel their hugs. I am grateful to AA and to my Higher Power, whom I chose to call God, that I have been given this wonderful program for living that guides me daily. I am grateful to be able to tell my children that I love them.

It's an Inside Job
JD M.

I arrived at rehab because of a problem with drugs. After decades of using various forms of "recreational" chemicals, which I had always been able to stop when things got too bad, I had finally met my match with crack cocaine.

I agreed to treatment mainly because I needed a rest. I'd been using heavily for well over a year, eventually holed up in my house trying to run my business by telephone and avoiding direct contact with colleagues, friends and family. Long runs of sleepless days and nights had left me exhausted. I felt hopeless.

After several weeks of treatment, I was refreshed and ready to go home and carry on with my life. If I just didn't pick up the first one, I'd be okay — how hard could that be? After all, I'd had many periods of abstinence in the past. I had good willpower and was particularly motivated — and I'd resolved never to go near crack again; that's for sure.

Long-term treatment had been recommended but I knew they were just after my cash and, besides, I had a life to catch up on. My counsellor had said that I had little or no chance of making it to a year. My peer group had voted me "least likely to succeed." Oh yeah? I'll show them!

Driven by my own stubbornness and defiance, I did go to meetings (128 in the first 90 days) and hung out with others in early recovery. But I was skeptical and scared of the "god thing" and thought the Twelve Steps were a scheme to convert me to religion. I thought that most of the other people I saw at meetings were losers.

That "program" kept me abstinent for the next few months. But the relative ease and relief I'd felt immediately after treatment eroded as time wore on and I began to dread a lifetime of abstinence.

Luckily, in my fifth month, I met an old-timer named Fred. I shared my anger and skepticism, particularly about having a spiritual experience — whatever that was. Fred listened patiently, then asked me to tell him about treatment. One story I told him was about a game we'd played, pushing coins across a table with funny names we'd made up for various shots, and how we'd laughed — some of us for the first time in years.

Fred stopped me at that point and asked how I had felt when we laughed. At first, I wasn't sure what he meant. With his prompting, I was able to say that in those moments, I had felt happy and connected with my fellow addicts. Fred said that what I'd had was a spiritual experience. Oh.

He then asked me what it felt like when I had my first drink or toke. I told him about feeling at ease and being able to relate better to those around me. He said that these too were spiritual experiences. Oh.

Then he really got my attention. He told me that recovery wasn't just about abstinence — although that was a necessary start. It was about learning how to have spiritual experiences using healthy methods. He said I could learn how to deal with the fear and aloneness that had dogged me all my life.

Now that appealed to me! I was willing to work toward that. Since Fred seemed to know what he was talking about, I asked how he did it and he said he'd show me how.

He got me going with the basics. The only feelings I could readily identify were anger and elation. He asked me to try "sad, mad or glad." I struggled, but started to pay attention to what my body was telling me. Often it was painful — but Fred assured me it would get better. He said that my job was to experience the feelings, to "make them my friends," and to watch that I didn't act out in harmful or destructive ways.

This was the hardest thing I'd ever done. I had been raised in a family and in a community where feelings were taboo and to admit any weakness was just asking for trouble. I felt embarrassed and ashamed.

But, with Fred's support, I started to listen to others share about their feelings and to realize I was not alone. I started to experience a sense of connection and belonging. Just what Fred had promised.

Since then, my recovery journey has deepened and broadened. I still have times where I feel my guts in a knot, where I experience fear and sadness. But they don't scare me now. I know they will pass. I don't have to numb my feelings with chemicals or act out in harmful, shameful ways.

Best of all, at times I experience a quiet bliss, a connection to and compassion for others. And by sharing my experience, strength and hope, I may become someone else's Fred.

Trusting the Voice Inside

Helen P. (Family Program)

Dealing with addiction is not like dealing with anything else; it takes a whole new set of tools. No wonder we need the help of something/someone greater than ourselves. When dealing with a loved one in the grips of addiction, it's not like dealing with a rational, sane person. There is a twisted darkness and incomprehensible quality to it.

I have been married for 15 years to a man I love and admire. Though he has been a heavy drinker throughout the time I have known him, I started to see signs of the addiction taking hold in the last year and a half. This included personality changes: becoming more argumentative, morose and withdrawn. He denied that the alcoholism was the cause of our problems, but rather that tensions in the marriage were causing him to drink more. Eventually, for my own sanity and to stabilize our home situation for my daughter, I asked my husband to leave our home and stay out until he went to treatment.

With support from Al-Anon, I have begun to make better choices. My husband is working to quit drinking on his own but has not entered treatment. I have had to work at practicing detachment and re-focusing my attention on my life and my daughter.

When I am struggling and trying to make sense of this twisted world of addiction, it really helps to ground myself with this question: "How do I want to show up today?" Not in response to anyone or to any circumstances, just, "How do I want to show up today?" Because I have a child, this question is even more motivating as it helps me take responsibility to bring the best to my daughter.

When I think of it this way, I have less anxiety when I tell my husband that I won't take money out of emergency savings for him to spend. At first, I was scared to set this boundary. When I thought about him I felt scared that he would be angry with me, and sad that he would suffer. But then I thought, How do I want to show up for my daughter? If I transfer those funds, I will be fearful, anxious and stressed. I will not be able to be present and available to her.

This made my decision clear: I needed to set this limit so I could show up how I want to, both for me and for my daughter. Sometimes it's hard to hear the answer to that question when anxiety and resentment run high. That's what slogans, readings, meetings and prayer are for: to quiet the noise so you can hear the soft little answer inside.

When I think of my husband, I think he has a big, loud bullying voice inside his head: the voice of his addiction. This makes it impossible for him to hear his own little voice or anyone else's at times. Maybe it's because of this that addicts must see and experience the consequences of their actions in order to believe for themselves — because they can't trust the voice inside.

I find it takes a lot of discipline and practice to refocus on myself, but using the tools of hearing, trusting and acting on the voice inside is my best chance for a healthy future for me and my family.

Learning to Start Living Again

Curtis T. (Punanai 2011)

When I left Renascent, it was suggested by my sponsor and many other people in the program that I should move into a sober living environment. I told my sponsor that I would think about it. A person who I really looked up to in the program at the time was living at Alpha House and had nothing but positive things to say about the house and the staff. Back then, Alpha House had a solid group of guys who would go around together to all the different meetings, which I thought was really cool.

At first, I hated the idea of being back in a structured environment where I would have to do chores, have a curfew and be accountable to people. So when I left Renascent, I moved back into my mom's place where I had been living before I went into treatment. This was a place where I did a lot of my drinking and using. A place where I spent a lot of time alone. At first, things went very well. A month sober, getting back on track, a new beginning. But after a few weeks, the glitz and glamour of being newly sober started to wear off. My mom and I started to get on each other's nerves.

I soon realized I had fallen back into old thought patterns and some old behaviours. It was very eerie sleeping and waking up in the same bed that I had been in while I was out there. It didn't help that I didn't have a job at the time, had a smoking habit and had to constantly nag my mom for everything.

Within a few weeks, it was clear that I had to move out. Not just for my recovery but also for my mom and her well-being. Around this time, I heard different speakers talking about how much Alpha House helped their recovery. I was especially inspired by a few long timers (20+ years) sharing about their experience and how much they had learned and benefited from living in a recovery home during their early sobriety.

That's when it was decided that a recovery home would be best for me. I would move into Alpha House. While I was on the waiting list,

I was told to call the house every day, which I did, and also attend the in-house meetings, which I did. Soon enough I was in.

It took some getting used to at first to go from my mom's place to a house with 15 guys and a staff. It took some adjusting, too, to go from no structure to structure. But it was great. I was now surrounded by people in recovery. It was then that I started to learn how to live in and be a part of a community. At Alpha House, I learned to set goals, cook, clean, live with other people and a whole lot of other life skills that I still use to this day. After about five months, I was told I should start looking for a new place. I didn't want to leave, but it was time to move on. From Alpha I moved into St. Vincent de Paul.

Recovery homes for me have been life-changing. Being with other people in recovery around the clock and having a safe place to go in early recovery is priceless. I can't imagine my sobriety if I had not gone. When I talk to new guys, I try to always tell them about my experience in these kinds of homes to hopefully inspire them to do the same. It's difficult to articulate just how good these homes are for people in recovery, because of how bad we want to just be back out on our own and make up for lost time.

For me, what I have gotten out of these places is more valuable than gold. These homes gave me a place where I could learn to start living again.

A Journey to Myself

Nicolle N.

As I sit down to write this article, on the table in front of me lie my journals from this past year.

They are different colours and sizes, some given to me as gifts, some bought in a dollar store and one from a professional office supply store. No matter what the cost, they are precious to me, as are the two people who suggested to me many years ago: "Nicolle, why don't you start a journal?"

One of those people was my sponsor, Leslie. I was having a great deal of difficulty with prayer and surrender, and it was Leslie who said if I was having a hard time, to open up my journal and just try talking to my Higher Power. I was 22 years old when I got sober and I remember saying, "But I don't even really know my Higher Power yet!"

Leslie also asked me if I would be willing to use my journal to write down affirmations and a gratitude list. I think I said I would be, but I knew in my heart that I had no faith whatsoever in affirmations or journal writing at that time. But I listened and I was willing. The first affirmation Leslie suggested I write in my journal was "I am a sober woman of dignity and worth."

Soon I began to get up in the morning, pray and write, focusing on simple affirmations and simple statements of what I was grateful for. At first, it felt empty and foreign. My sponsor suggested that maybe that was because for the first time I was developing a real and honest relationship with myself.

Journaling was difficult for me because it took time, commitment and nurturing energy; all things that I found difficult to give to myself but desperately needed. It was through the practice of keeping a journal that I began my journey to a better and lasting relationship with a Higher Power and with myself.

Another important person in my life who suggested that I keep a journal was my counsellor at that time. Being newly sober, I sometimes felt overwhelmed by the feelings that were emerging. I needed to learn how to identify and cope with my feelings. He encouraged me to start writing down thoughts and feelings, so that I might increase my awareness and ability to cope.

I found this frightening. It was a new freedom that I wasn't too sure how to deal with, but he helped me to move through my fears. If I was having difficulty or fear, or if I was stuck and unable to face my feelings, especially the negative ones, he suggested that I grab some scissors and a magazine and find a picture or colour that helped to capture the essence of my feeling.

This really opened me up. I was also relieved to discover that journal writing wasn't about my writing having to be "perfect," "neat" or "intellectual." I was given permission to make my journal my own. He suggested that I cut out images, use stickers, design my own cover or doodle with markers. The next thing I knew, I was having fun! What a miracle! Having fun while working on myself!

He also recommended a book called The Artist's Way by Julia Cameron, which explores many suggestions to open up one's creative expression, including the practice of what she calls "Morning Pages." I know that I needed help to create a more positive daily life in sobriety, of which journaling was a big part. I began to trust and to listen to myself a bit more. I felt more balanced and I began to trust that there were possibilities for fun, joy and happiness in a sober life.

Today, for me, 14 and half years sober (one day at a time), journaling is an essential tool that I rely on; a quiet, intimate time devoted to my recovery and my Higher Power. In times of emotional stress, it grounds me so that I can stop and practice the slogans "Easy Does It" and "Keep It Simple." It helps me to sort out my busy mind and to identify fears, resentments and changes that I might need help with. It helps me to work the Steps with my sponsor.

It also helps me to identify positive goals and dreams for my sobriety. Oftentimes, I go back and re-read my journal and look for when I am saying the same thing over and over. This can be an indication to me that I need help in this area.

For me, writing is a regular, daily practice just as prayer is. Both have a positive effect on my emotional sobriety and serenity.

I have so much to be grateful for. How thankful I am to have been given the opportunity to share a little bit of my recovery with you. It seems fitting somehow that in this moment, I lack the "right" words to describe the depth of gratitude and the sense of wonder and awe I feel for the power of this program.

Maybe a colour would best describe the feeling: a bright, warm yellow and gold colour that cuts mysteriously through every dark nook and cranny, and amazingly beams strong, brilliant light and warmth everywhere.

Happy journaling!

We Are Not a Glum Lot

Paul S. (Punanai 2011)

We've been there — the after-work gathering with its impromptu patio patter, unwinding after a rough day, laughing at each other, gossiping, tossing barbs at those not present, back patting, flirting, telling bad jokes, all the while hoisting, sipping, and slurping adult beverages of every colour and shape. Oh, the civility, the pomp, the ritual, the oh-so-adultness of it all. We feel that somehow we have arrived. We let alcohol give us the warm and fuzzies as we progress into more jocularity and perhaps delve into deep metaphysical discussions in the corner.

For most non-alcoholics, it usually doesn't go much further than this. They pack up their handbags, their backpacks and their briefcases and motor on home. For alcoholics of my type, that doesn't cut it. We, of course, need to go blotting out our own existence and drinking into oblivion and getting into a drunken stupor that eliminates us from being in our own skin. Most often, we do that on our own and alone, once everyone has gone home and continued to live normal lives.

Now, for us alcoholics, it wasn't always like that. There was a time when alcohol worked. There was a time when we could take it or leave it. I know there was a time when I could shut it down after a few drinks. I would not get wrapped up and hog-tied to booze and its effects. I could have those after-work/celebratory/leisurely drinks and then move on with my life. I could have those hearty laughs, that feeling of connection, that sense of well-being.

Of course it was an illusion, a false front, a side effect of the poison I was putting into my body. Not to say that having a few drinks doesn't loosen people up and give them a sense of fun. It certainly does, and it did for me, for a time. But at some point, I don't know when, I just crossed a line and I can never go back to those days. Ever.

Now, there is this sense that we recovering/recovered alcoholics are a dour set. That once we remove the "fun juice" from our lives, we are relegated to live a life of stone-cold dullness, of spinster-like dowdiness, of liver-healing boredom. We feel that we are the stone in the Shoe of Fun. We begin to believe that we will never ever feel a part of anything ever again. We feel that we no longer have what it takes to face those few folks from the office at quitting time, let alone the world as a whole. It feels as though we have been ripped away from the one thing that has kept us connected to the ground, to others and to the Universe.

And we have been, for the most part.

I wasn't a huge bar guy in the last few years of my drinking. I didn't socialize much. I didn't do the drinks after work thing. I drank alone. Secretively. So for this alcoholic, I never had a problem with the idea of not having fun at a party or gathering because, frankly, I stopped having fun a very long time ago. Even when I was drinking, I never had fun. I was too wrapped up in myself to enjoy the company of others. I didn't enjoy the company of me, so how I could I extend that to others?

I realize that for many of us, social gatherings are a problem once we sober up. Certainly, I had to avoid social gatherings for a short time, as I just needed to be away from any place that had alcohol. But for many alcoholics, one of the biggest first challenges is the get-together. Alcohol is almost always available, and indulged in, when a group gathers in the name of "fun." So we fuss and worry and struggle with how we are going to feel and, more importantly, what we think we are going to be seen as: The boring alkie. The soda-sucking sober gal. The teetotalling tosser in the corner.

This is pride talking. And it is, of course, hogwash.

Just because we sober up, doesn't mean that we've shut the door on connecting and laughing and being with others in a playful and light way. We don't turn into stone figures. We may feel like that for awhile, and certainly during very early recovery it feels like things will never turn around, but we start to plug into life in a whole different way. And one way of plugging in for me was going to meetings.

One of the great things about meetings is the camaraderie, the joy, the laughter that emanates from the rooms. For those who haven't had the experience of being in a roomful of drunks, it's quite amazing. We laugh when we hear about someone's arrest record, we giggle when we hear about the attempts at hiding bottles and street fights, we snort and chuckle when someone talks about the hospitalizations or the bankruptcies. To a non-alcoholic observer, they would be horrified to hear this, and worse, to see everyone else making light of it all. We find humour in it because we've been there before and are really laughing at ourselves.

Rule #62 — Don't take yourself so seriously.

"We are not a glum lot," the Big Book of Alcoholics Anonymous states. We don't get sober and recover to not enjoy life. Life is for living.

Recovery Love

Lynn A.

Love is a complex emotion and not easily described. We experience love in many ways and in varying degrees. I am writing to share my experience with "romantic" love and my first loving relationship ever sober!

During my first year of sobriety, I was told by many, "don't get involved in a romantic relationship in your first year." Being naturally defiant, I wanted to go against what I was told, and if the "perfect" person appeared, I might have jumped at the chance. Thankfully, once again, God knew better than I did.

As the fog lifted and my perception became closer to the truth, I realized that what people were telling me was to help me, not control me. As my trust in God grew, I naturally accepted the loving relationships that were presented to me and I started to develop true love, first with God and myself, my family and my friends. As my understanding of love grew, I was no longer seeking romantic love; I was complete as I was.

Most people think of not having a relationship as not having sex for an entire year! I know, it sounds scary!

As part of my Step work and self-searching, I completed a "sexual" inventory and took a look at my past actions and how I perceived intimacy. I did as instructed and completed "an ideal" and I asked God to help me live up to what was more in line with who I am. Loving myself includes respecting myself. I am not a saint, nor did I take an oath of celibacy. I knew that if the situation was presented, I would ask God to direct me. In terms of where to find this, look to the following in the Big Book of Alcoholics Anonymous (pages 69–70):

> *We asked God to mold our ideals and help us to live up to them.*

In meditation, we ask God what we should do about each specific matter.

To sum up about sex: We earnestly pray for the right ideal, for guidance in each questionable situation, for sanity, and for the strength to do the right thing.

After a few more years, the day finally came ... I made a connection with someone, unlike any other I'd ever had. It was an "energetic" feeling that took over; it was a powerful energy source that was overwhelming. At that exact moment, I knew why this person wasn't presented to me in early recovery. It was consuming. Like a drug, it took over my thoughts, my feelings, my appetite, my sleep, my world. I felt real love for the first time.

I knew from my experience with loving others and myself that with this new-found love, I would need to apply the same actions — honesty, open communication, trust, intimacy, loyalty, truth, affection, respect, patience, tolerance and understanding. I also learned that love, like recovery, is work and it's not something I can take for granted. Acceptance and expectations also have to be applied. Today, the person I love is aligned spiritually — we are not of the same faith and our Gods are not the same, but our respect for each other's choices allows us to be aligned.

It has not been easy, it's not perfect and it has also come with challenges throughout our time together. When I am feeling discontent, I am aware that the problem is me and that I'm having expectations or thinking of past experiences that I think may play out, so I need to remember to remind myself, "I am human and love is a gift"; that God has chosen this person to help me learn and grow; that our gifts for each other are not material items, they are patience, respect and tolerance; and that sometimes it's not about what I need, it's about what my partner needs to learn and grow.

The beauty of my love story is that it's ever-changing, it has deepened and evolved, and it has only just begun.

That's Progress!
Randy M.

Like all of the Al-Anon slogans, "Progress, not perfection" seems on first consideration to be a mere catchphrase. But after more than 10 years of growth and healing in the program, I have come to rely on it as my working principle: it, as well as the other slogans, gives me the encouragement and endurance I need to work every Step and Tradition.

It was confirmed to me only a couple of years ago that my maternal grandfather was an alcoholic (the only problem drinker in the family as far as I know). He passed away when I was nine years old. Inevitably, my mother and family were affected by the disease.

Early on, I came to crave the approval of other people and to dread their disapproval, to the extent that I based everything I would say or do on an internal calculation of the risk of having someone think I was "bad." I was often fearful of trying potentially beneficial new things. My desire for perfection foreclosed the possibility of any progress. During the worst stretches of this insanity, I felt like I was living my life as if I couldn't wait to get it over with safely.

After years of aimless living and one failed marriage, I eventually — perhaps inevitably — married an alcoholic. For that, I am truly grateful, not only for our continuing loving commitment to each other, but also because she was my "ticket in" to the Al-Anon fellowship, as I saw it then. In retrospect, I could easily have qualified for Alateen many years ago, but that doesn't matter now. Thanks to the program, I'm not so big on "retrospect" anymore — nor on fearful anxiety for the future, for that matter!

The "Progress, not perfection" slogan covers every aspect of recovery, but here I will confine myself to how it has helped me to "let go and let God." Before I came to Al-Anon, my personal belief in a benevolent Higher Power was only lip service and wishful thinking. Even so, however, there were times when I hit bottom hard enough that I could only surrender, which is to say: (i) stop trying to affect outcomes that never were in my control, and (ii) humbly pray for strength and guidance. That is when my miracle would happen without fail, albeit usually in an entirely unexpected way.

I didn't learn from those experiences, however. Every such time, I would feel great temporary relief but promptly revert to the futile manipulative behaviour and procrastination that had served me so badly for so long. Then I began working the Steps, sharing with a sponsor and with my Al-Anon friends, and being of service. I soon learned that when it comes to anything except my own attitudes and actions, "giving up" is not a last resort, but should be practised consciously, as best as I can in the moment given to me.

In time, through this practice, I truly did come to believe in a Higher Power who could restore me to sanity. How so? Because miracles continued to happen whenever I let go and let God.

Just as I no longer expect that things in general will work out "perfectly," and no longer go into paralysis if perfection can't be guaranteed, I don't pressure myself to work my program perfectly. From time to time, I still find myself grasping for control of the uncontrollable, particularly when there is a strong emotional charge for me in the outcome, but I do so less frequently than before and I am much the happier for it. That's progress!

I do not expect to "graduate" from Al-Anon. It is, exactly as it promises, a spiritual program, and when it comes to things of the spirit, not even the sky is the limit.

Keep coming back.

A Mugful of Humility

Dale H. (Walker 1995)

I knew I was in the right place when I heard another alcoholic share that he had both a superiority complex and an inferiority complex. That described how I'd felt all my life! Smarter than other people, but defective in some way. Always an outsider, thinking I was better than and less than, all at the same time. Drinking was the only thing that made me feel remotely the same as other people.

So I was pretty confused when we started talking about humility during my stay at Renascent. I realized I didn't even know what the word meant. Out came the office dictionary.

I read: "Humility is derived from the Latin *humilitas*; that which is abject, ignoble, or of poor condition." I thought, Well, I already think this about myself. I already think I'm a loser; that there's something terribly wrong and defective about me. I can't possibly have a humility problem, so this Step really doesn't apply to me.

So much for Step Seven!

A couple of days later, I decided to buy a traveller's coffee mug so I could take decaf coffee to the evening meetings we attended. Since we were restricted to a one-block radius whenever we left the house, the only place to buy a mug was the Coffee Time across the street.

They had the ugliest coffee mugs I'd ever seen. I was a Starbucks girl, don't you know! I wanted something stainless steel, smooth and reeking of coolness. Yet here I was, my only option a huge white plastic abomination with a red lid, red handle and "Coffee Time" emblazoned across it in the brightest, sickliest of reds. Even the girl behind the counter agreed that it was too ugly for words.

I thought to myself, I can't take this mug to AA meetings! What will people think? They'll know I'm a loser. They'll think I have no money, no taste, no culture, no esthetic discernment. People will think I'm … I'm low class! I was in a dilemma. It was this mug or no mug — but I couldn't possibly buy this horrible thing!

And then a moment of clarity hit me like a brick: how arrogant I was to think that all those people in the AA meeting were going to be looking at, and thinking about, me and my coffee mug! I saw that this was ego, pure and simple. I suddenly realized that nobody in the darn meeting was likely to notice or care what kind of coffee mug I had at all. They weren't all sitting there waiting for my entrance, analyzing my every move. And I thought, Hmmm, maybe this is what they mean by humility.

So I bought it. I named it my "Humility Mug." I took it with me to the meeting that night and, sure enough, not one person gave me and my mug a withering glance of disapproval. No one noticed or cared. Not that night, or the next, or the 22 nights after that, or the next 10 years after that. No one gave me or my mug a second look.

I know it was just a coffee mug, but it represented so much more to me. For years, I'd thought that everyone in the world was judging me the way I judged myself — with absolutely no mercy. It would literally take me hours to get up the nerve to walk down Bloor Street for 10 minutes. I thought everyone was looking at me with disgust — that they saw how ugly I was, that I had no friends, that I was a loser. Those 10 minutes would seem like a lifetime and I would scurry back home to the safety of my apartment.

And now, in that moment of clarity, I realize that everyone wasn't looking at me. Everyone wasn't judging me. Everyone was thinking about themselves, not about me. I wasn't that important! And the feeling of freedom that I experienced then was indescribable.

I had had it all so wrong. Because I had felt so terrible about myself, I assumed I couldn't have an ego problem. But I discovered that thinking you're the worst is just as egotistical as thinking you're the best. The truth is, I'm just one of many. I'm just a human being like everyone else — no better, no worse. Knowing I'm no worse helped me to develop a sense of self-worth. And knowing I'm no better helped me accept that there just might be a power in this universe greater than me!

Whichever way you look at it, to me it means freedom from self. This is why my favourite prayer is the Third Step prayer, where I ask to be relieved of the bondage of self. An over-exaggerated sense of self continues to be at the root of all my difficulties.

The freedom of humility remains one of the most priceless gifts of recovery for me. I know that 99% of the time what people do and say has absolutely nothing to do with me, even if it's directed at me. It's almost always about them. And if it is about me, I can take responsibility for it — and hopefully learn from it — without thinking I'm a horrible person. I no longer feel a need to be superior or inferior to anyone.

This knowledge leaves me free to be me, whomever that might be. It takes the weight of the world off my shoulders. I don't have to be thinking about me and what people think of me, or what I think about them, all the time.

The burdens of self-importance and self-obsession are heavy ones. I want to travel lightly through the world now. Humility is the gift that lightens my step.

"Non-doing" is Hard to Do!

George L. (Punanai 2006)

First things first! I'm delighted and honored to have the privilege of writing for this newsletter. Thanks to the Twelve Steps of recovery, I just celebrated nine months of continuous sobriety and clean time. I spent last Christmas and New Year's at Renascent's Punanai Centre in Toronto and, in short, it saved my life.

I'll be forever grateful to the staff, the counsellors, my sponsor, my fellow graduates, my blood family and my extended new family throughout the city's many AA and CA fellowships. Their wisdom and support have given this addict a second chance and I plan to make the most of it by living clean and serving others.

On to the topic of this essay, "Time Management in Early Recovery." I don't know about the rest of you, but in the first few months of my recovery, time was "the enemy"! Having stopped so abruptly decades of living a life predicated on drugs and alcohol made me subject to risk — but more than that, I was bored out of my mind!

In those first three months, it wasn't so much that I craved booze and dope as much as I craved a distraction from the routine of recovery. Time often seemed to flow in slow motion. Without my ex-wife, home, car or job to fill the time between meetings, I sometimes swore that the hands on the clock were frozen or even going backwards.

Jerry Seinfeld said in a recent New York Times Magazine, "People say life is too short when it's actually too long. Malls and coffee shops prove it — they exist solely to drain off time!" (And boy, oh boy, do we know coffee shops!)

On the flip side, life and technology seem to be speeding up exponentially. Processing daily information and keeping up with the pace of modern society — even for this unemployed, unattached 40-year-old — can sometimes be very trying.

For most of my "using" career, I held a high-profile job as an on-air television personality; the last seven of those years in a newsroom where "Time is King." Working to deadlines was an obsession and maximizing time through years of multi-tasking and training became second nature for me.

This spilled over into my addictions as well, to the point where I was always playing catch-up with fellow addicts and then with myself as I isolated over the last two years of heavy use.

One of the greatest gifts of my recovery has been the introduction of prayer and meditation into my life. Just to be clear, I'm nowhere near where I'd like to be on this front yet, but I am working on it. Thanks to the open-minded nature of this program and the encouragement of my sister, who throws a wide range of spiritual literature my way, I have begun to study in the "classroom of silence" for the first time in my life.

I'm currently on Step Eleven in my recovery and I try to put aside 10 to 15 minutes at the top or bottom of each day to just sit still and be. It is still hard for me to practice what the Buddhists call "non-doing" — the domain of true meditation.

The way I approach it is to sit upright and motionless in my quiet, third floor attic bedroom or on the adjacent outdoor deck, which offers sunlight and the relaxing sounds of birds, breeze and the light hum of Bloor Street a block away. While breathing deeply and counting backwards from 100 to 0, I try to place myself on a quiet beach walking back and forth between the ocean and a nearby garden filled with butterflies and various woodland critters.

If this sounds flaky, so be it! It was a technique introduced to me at Renascent's excellent aftercare program and I find it most useful in helping me to clear my mind of the daily clutter. Rather than worrying about doing nothing, I try to concentrate on the fact that nothing important is being left undone.

Without the chaos of a full-time addiction to drag me down, I am free to enjoy my own company again. Free to realize that the only time I really have is now even though we live in a world that tries very hard to convince us otherwise. Success is the fruit of *discipline*, something I had lost all connection with during my years of addiction.

I now have the humility to accept my current situation and the clarity and conviction to work for a better tomorrow. I can now make plans without "living" in them as I used to. The basic tools of recovery that I learned at Renascent help me manage the hours of each day much better than before. Getting enough sleep, eating properly and regularly, washing, exercising and — most importantly — *not* isolating have allowed me to rejoin society.

My goal for the future is to be useful. Success will follow. "Yesterday is history, tomorrow is a mystery, today is a gift ... which is why we call it the present."

"Face Everything And Recover"

Nancy L. (Munro 2005)

F.E.A.R. — F... EVERYTHING AND RUN: how I dealt with fear before entering a program of recovery.

F.E.A.R. — FACE EVERYTHING AND RECOVER: how I've learned in recovery to deal with fear now.

I first heard these acronyms in an AA meeting when I was about nine months into my first year. I heard them and of course simply filed them away.

It wasn't too many days later when I was presented with something I didn't want to handle. I knew enough to know that alcohol, my old friend in these sticky situations, wasn't there for me now. What to do? Not to worry — I'd simply ignore the problem!

Then it started to gnaw on my conscience. It was still a day away. I started to worry about what would happen if I ignored it. Then I started to sweat. It certainly wasn't a nice feeling. Well, a small lie would be okay, too — that should take the pressure off. For the next few hours, I was thinking of the pros and cons of doing or not doing something. I skipped dinner. I was too busy worrying to be hungry.

"Face Everything And Recover" popped up in my mind. Should I? Somehow, just thinking of this as a possibility made me feel better. Okay, I'd give it a try. Wonder of wonders, I got hungry. I ate, read some of my Big Book, and turned off the light with a determination that I was going to give it a try.

The next day, I faced the confrontation, which I was sure would go badly. It didn't. Words came to my lips that simply amazed me. I was honest. I didn't tell a lie. I simply said what was on my mind and answered questions truthfully. I walked away with a simply indescribable feeling of warmth.

That was my first inclination that this AA program may have something to it. I talked with my sponsor about what had just happened. It was made clear to me that although I did face my fear, in doing so I had done something that I could have never done in the past.

"How did that happen?" my sponsor asked. Yes, I did the work by facing it, but something gave me the strength to do it. "Something greater than you?" asked my sponsor. A light was starting to glow in this old mind of mine. I could see a direct correlation between a real situation in my life, and something greater than me helping me. My sponsor and I used this experience to start my Step Two journey.

Over the next few weeks, as always, I had lots of things I didn't want to do. "Procrastination" was my middle name and I used that liberally whenever I could. However, there were some things I couldn't put off. Each time I either started to get that old gut feeling of impending doom or started to sweat and shake. When the pain got bad enough, the words "Face Everything And Recover" popped up. I faced many things and the negative projections I'd foreseen did not happen.

Okay, this was bugging me. What was happening, and why the pain? One word, my sponsor said, "Fear." I sort of knew that, and I knew that was the acronym I'd been using, but what was this fear? My sponsor and I had been working on Step Three for a while by this time, and I was getting quite comfortable that something was indeed helping me get through life's issues. Time for Step Four, my sponsor told me. The Big Book tells us that we have to follow Step Three with "action" — Step Four.

So I took action. I did my inventory (Step Four) and discussed it with my sponsor (Step Five). I learned that most of my life was driven by fear. I found out that the words read at meetings from our AA literature definitely applied to me. I was constantly worried about losing something I had or not getting something that I wanted. Wow! That was all news to me, but my sponsor pointed out that all this was really great news. We now had something to work with (my character defects) and tools to fix me (the Twelve Steps).

With help from my Higher Power, my life started to change. I now had some concrete behaviours that I could change. I started using

FEAR as a positive thing in my life. It was now a wonderful feeling when I started to be upset or when I began to feel frightened. What was I frightened of? Well, the details were always a bit different, but it always fell into one of these two categories: not getting something I wanted or losing something I already had.

But now I had a solution. I didn't have to face this alone — I had a Higher Power. This allowed me to face my fears. But I also had a new way of looking at the root cause of those fears, and with that information I could work on myself.

It's taking me some time, but I'm finally starting to become a Grateful Alcoholic. My life is becoming something of a dream world, full of the dreams I had long ago that seemed to be impossible before I came into recovery. And I'm now becoming the kind of person I've always seen in others, but never dreamed that I could be.

I'm changing, not because my life is more manageable, but because when things happen I'm facing them with my Higher Power. That's where the thanks belong.

"Face Everything And Recover" — words that help me get through my FEARS.

A Man in Need of a Psychic Change

Alex H. (Punanai 2003)

There was a time in my life when *the absolute best* behaviour I was capable of was substandard and generally harmful to other people around me. I was completely self-absorbed, felt very low on the character scale and was beginning to notice an increasing sense of hopelessness.

I had but one solution: hiding out in what I thought was the "comfort" I found in my addiction to cocaine, complemented by the "warmth" I imagined I experienced after each ounce of vodka I swallowed.

As is usually the case with addicts of my type, the substances that helped me to feel normal and sane began to turn on me. I needed more of them to feel the same imaginary relief. The incessant need I had to continuously change the way I felt became completely overpowering. As a result, the behaviours I engaged in to actually get alcohol and drugs grew increasingly more inappropriate with each passing day.

I became a liar. I stole from people I loved and who loved me back. I became completely unpredictable, unreliable and unwelcome in every area of my life.

Those who loved me all thought I was going to die, and that was starting to seem okay with me in my narrow little world of self-pity. I figured I was better off dead, anyway. At least all the hurt I was causing them would go away.

Two treatment centres and a few years of sobriety later, I know today that my problems back then were not the alcoholism or the addiction. Those were quite obviously *problematic*, but they were not the driving force that was making my life seem so terrible.

During treatment and in my attempts at sobriety that followed, I had been made aware of the idea that my problem generally centred on the fact that the way I thought about and perceived the world was flawed.

At first, that was a foreign and somewhat offensive proposition for a man of my imaginary intellectual calibre. I was a guy who believed my own hype. I thought I was generally a cut above most, if not all, of the people I initially met in the rooms of recovery. I instantaneously compared myself to everyone around me, and failed to identify with what they were saying about the solution they had been given to our common disease of addiction.

In essence, my flawed thinking and flawed perception of myself and the world around me stopped me from being able to hear what I needed to do: change the very device that was keeping me sick — my mind. I was a man very much in need of a psychic change.

After a 14-month period of relapsing and pretending to others that I was remaining sober, I began to feel a hopelessness far greater than the one I had come to know a couple of years previously. This time felt different, though, because now I was in a constant state of shame.

People were telling me, based on the misinformation I was giving them, that they were proud of me and happy that I had chosen to live in recovery. My absolute best thinking brought me to a place in my life where absolutely every relationship I had was based on a lie.

That was my bottom.

It was the spiritual death I felt inside of me that enabled me to accept that I was a very sick person who desperately needed a new outlook on life. It was a moment of clarity that showed me that the problem was of my own doing, and that I couldn't undo it on my own. It was the time that I completely understood that I needed to dramatically change what was going on in my thinking so that I could start living life in a loving, productive and useful way. It was then that I realized that I first needed to stop lying to myself before I could stop lying to everybody else.

Those beautiful people in the rooms of recovery I had so wrongly accused of being "worse" than me were waiting for me with open arms to show me the solution I very much needed. I got over my self-imposed superiority and asked them for help. The despair I felt helped me to humble myself enough to be able to look past how they appeared and instead listen to what they said.

Those words I heard each night in the rooms of Alcoholics Anonymous and Cocaine Anonymous helped my Higher Power save my life, because they gave me hope. They gave me a reason to come back the next night and listen to the next message I needed to hear.

By showing up regularly, I was given the gift of true friends and an opportunity to build real relationships with them. In doing that, I was able to understand how to re-build relationships with my own loved ones, whom I had hurt so much in the darkness of my addictions.

My view of life used to cause me pain. My pain caused me to seek relief and I found it in alcohol and drugs. Alcohol and drugs took my already-dangerous thinking and made it even sicker, bringing me to a place far more pitiful and painful than I ever thought possible. That place broke me and gave me a willingness to seek an alternative, healthier solution.

I found recovery, and by taking the simple actions outlined to me by people who were already living in the solution, I found a life that I wanted and is definitely worth living!

To Thine Own Self Be True

Susan R. (Munro 1999)

> *This above all: to thine own self be true,*
> *And it must follow, as the night the day,*
> *Thou canst not then be false to any man.*
> *William Shakespeare*

When I think about "self-respect," the wise quotation from Shakespeare's Hamlet, "To thine own self be true," comes racing into my mind. Before recovery I had very little, if any, proper respect for myself. Who had the time for self-respect?

While active in the disease of alcoholism, the only thing I was "true" to was alcohol and the pursuit of it. Then, towards the end of my drinking, I couldn't spend 90 days outside of some kind of institution — hospital, detox, psychiatric establishment or doctor's office to name a few.

There were periods where I was, shall we say, "undomiciled" (homeless). During these episodes, or crises, self-respect was not high on my "to do" list. I didn't like myself at all. Maybe you can relate.

And, when I think about "self-esteem," I remember that in the last years of being enslaved by alcohol, I became a professional victim. I felt so bad about "me," since I was a failure, that I no longer took responsibility for much at all, never mind myself.

I can recall helpful souls along the way diagnosing me with low self-esteem, and I would wonder how the heck I was supposed to understand low self-esteem when, by my account, I didn't have any self-esteem at all. Plus, all things being equal, when you don't feel like you have any of something, low sounds pretty good by comparison. It all depends on where you are coming from. When you don't have a home, self-esteem seems like a silly thing to be wanting for.

The diagnoses and advice from such helpers thus fell by the wayside and I continued to use alcohol to solve my problems. Instead of self-respect, I felt guilt, false pride and shame about my actions and behaviour.

Paradoxically though (and so much of this program of recovery seems to be paradoxical), all I did while drinking was think of me; just not in very high regard, apparently. Alcoholics are, after all, extremely self-centred and I was no different. So there I was, a garden-variety alcoholic, self-obsessed to the extreme, with low self-esteem and little or no self-respect.

Clearly, I was the last one to know all this about myself at that time.

Today, I am proud because I can say things are different, and that's putting it mildly. It has been a long time since I felt the kind of self-loathing that I lived with day in and day out while drinking, or the demoralization and despair.

For me, recovery began at Renascent. Renascent offered me a solution to my alcohol problem through example and this was a compelling lesson for me. They taught me that by believing in others, I could finally start believing in myself. That, in turn, released me from the self-hatred I had endured for so many years. Renascent helped me help myself! And I have never looked back.

By joining a 12-step home group and getting a sponsor, I began my journey into working the Steps of the program of recovery. By simply showing up, I was participating and I became connected. By taking action in my home group, I became a part of something bigger than myself and I let people get to know me. I came to believe in a higher power, and to believe in myself, one day at a time.

The direct result of practicing this design for living has been that I have been able to heal and, in so doing, have reclaimed my life. Gradually, yet steadily, I have developed a modicum of self-respect.

Practicing self-respect in my life today has a lot to do with my relationships with others. It is about teaching myself and others how I would like to be treated. As I respect myself, I now also try to respect others. They, in turn, respect me the same way.

This is an invaluable lesson for me because I always rubbed the world the wrong way and vice versa. But, through the Serenity Prayer at first, I discovered that if I am going to live with some peace of mind, I must resign myself to the ways of the world and accept people, places and things that I cannot change. What I can change is myself, my thinking and my feelings.

After all, recovery for me, in a nutshell, is about being good to God's kids and I am, despite myself, one of God's kids!

From Amorphous Me to Authentic Me

Rick J.

When I was in high school on an overnight excursion, I participated in a personality test activity. I was instructed to answer a large number of questions about myself. I was 18 years old.

When the results were distributed the next day, I was confused. My classmates were receiving results that were predominantly complimentary, while my results stated that my dominant personality trait was "amorphous." I didn't know what it meant, so I asked. I was told that it meant I had no particular form or structure.

I was flattered. I thought it was a good thing, an asset, actually. I thought that it meant I was flexible and adapted well.

The group leader, in front of all of my classmates, assured me that it was quite the opposite: that I didn't know who I was and that I took my shape from people and situations around me. I was speechless as the searing sting of shame and embarrassment shot through me. It hurt, but it was true.

As I grew older, this trait became more pronounced. When I would find myself in a new group or new situation, I would act very much like a fly on the wall, scouting out the room. I would be very quiet and withdrawn as I took the time I needed to figure out the "character" of the group or situation.

Was it loud, outgoing, quiet, respectful, serious or lighthearted? Whatever it was, I would adopt that character so that I could feel like I fit in. It was hard work, but it was all I knew how to do.

I am reminded of a movie I once saw where a woman was putting a puzzle together with the aid of a nail file. If the puzzle piece didn't fit where she wanted it to go, she would shave the piece until it did. Where it was really meant to go was irrelevant. Its authentic shape didn't matter. All that mattered was that it fit where she wanted it to!

This is a great metaphor for how I lived my life for many years. I would shave myself into all kind of shapes just to have the feeling that I fit. It never quite worked. The belief that I had to change to fit in was totally an illusion, but it was all I had at the time. I didn't know who I was and neither did anyone else.

I grew up in alcoholism. I was affected by the disease. Nobody ever told me that I was not good enough, but somewhere along the way, in the midst of the disease, I picked up that belief. I yearned to be a part of, but never truly felt that I was.

Each time that I "shape shifted" I reaffirmed my erroneous belief that who I was was not good enough. It was a vicious behaviour that wreaked havoc with my self-esteem, my social interactions and all of my relationships. Isolation became a self-prescribed cure.

Twenty years ago, at the end of a short and futile marriage, I sought help in Al-Anon. My wife's drinking had flipped me totally upside down. I had tried everything to keep her from leaving. It was exhausting and, in the end, totally ineffectual. What I found in Al-Anon was a group of people who understood. I did not have to *pretend* to be okay, I *was* okay. Who I was *was* good enough.

I was told early in my recovery that I "needed to act [my] way into right thinking, not think [my] way into right action." When I finished doing my Fifth Step with my sponsor, I said to her that there was nothing I had not told her. Her response still reverberates in me to this very day. She said, "I love you more, because I know you better." I did not have to pretend to be someone else anymore.

This freedom was, and remains to this day, exhilarating. I discovered the joy in being real, in being authentic. The Twelve Steps, the Twelve Traditions and the Twelve Concepts, in concert with the loving acceptance I found in the Al-Anon fellowship, were all the tools I needed.

I could look at myself in the mirror and like the person I saw. I realized that I was the same person in all of my situations and interactions. There was one of me and he showed everywhere. Life stopped becoming hard work and became joyous. I enjoyed people like I never had before.

My participation in my work took on new dimensions. I was free to state my opinion without waiting to see what the popular opinion was. I could share my view on an issue even if it was the minority view.

I became genuinely interested in others and friendships blossomed. I became the first to extend a hand. I started to engage others in conversation and shared more freely about myself. I started looking people in the eye when speaking and listened more intently.

Silence with others became comfortable. Being real, being honest and being available slowly became my normal way of acting. It is freer and much more attractive than being fake, dishonest and aloof.

Gone is the fear of being discovered for who I really am, because who I really am is out there for all to see. The amorphous me has been replaced with the authentic me and I am thankful to God, the program, the fellowship and my sponsor for the change.

Peeking Through Joy's Window

Paul S. (Punanai 2011)

My five-year-old son loves to run. Not just in a playful kind of run that little kids engage in, but in a divinely inspired kind of run that shows that he *loves* to run. He tires out well-conditioned nannies and caregivers (including me), can outrun and outlast kids almost twice his age, and he just never seems to fatigue. He smiles all the while. He's half legs, half goofy grin.

The other night, he was running down a hotel hallway towards the elevator. I, my wife and our three-year-old tried to keep up. When we did, my wife turned to the now-panting eldest and said, "Y, I think when you run, you are closest to God," and gave him a peck on the top of his head. And while, at the time, I didn't think much of that comment, it was only today, slowly, that it started to seep into my soul — those powerful words playing in the shadows of my mind. They have really resounded in me.

When I think of my son running, I feel the true happiness it gives him. It's like his spirit does soar, even if for a moment or two. I see that same soaring of spirit in my youngest when he discovers something again, but reacts as if it's his first time seeing or experiencing it. When he wrinkles his nose and bursts out with that great belly laugh of his, I feel that he is closest to God at that moment. It's like there is a brief, undisturbed, uncontrolled, unwavering, profound glimpse into *something* that we are privy to only in sacred moments. That *something* produces a light within us that exudes out towards others like a ripple in a pond, brushing up against us all without us knowing exactly what it is that has touched us. But we know that we have been touched.

That *something* is what I call Peeking Through Joy's Window.

I spent part of the day yesterday looking at others — people at work, on the streets, in cars — and wondering, what is it that they do that allows them to Peek Though Joy's Window? What is it underneath the uniforms, masks and façades of modern living that sends them to furtively glance through the Window? Do they even know that they are Peeking?

When I spy an old man navigating through a crowd with his walker, I often picture him as a young man, slapping his friends on the back, tugging at his girlfriend's sleeve, sneaking a kiss, playing at something that brings him close to something he approaches only when his mind and spirit are in alignment with the Creator's. What am I seeking when I look at that old man? Do I seek that very thing in myself?

When I was a young boy, there were things that I think had me Peeking Through Joy's Window. I can't really be sure; it's been such a long time. I used to read a lot, I listened to music, I played games, I was active in sports, I did karate like my uncle did. I loved homework and doing well in school. I enjoyed hanging out with adults and tried to act grown up and tried to mature faster. Why I was in a race to leapfrog over my childhood, I don't know. But there were good times. I had just blotted them out in my drinking — a natural consequence of trying to forget my past and present and destroy my future. Alcohol was like a huge magnet wiping out the remaining fading memories of my younger days.

I used to think that alcohol could bring me to a place of contentment, of bliss, of rapture. I could drink and actually feel what it was like to *feel*. I felt what it was like to be happy for once, to pick up the loving vibes from the room, to be lighter and stretched properly into my own skin. I truly felt that I was Peeking Through Joy's Window. But it was a façade. That Window I thought I was facing was only a picture of a Window — one-dimensional and quick to disappoint. Drinking brought me to the general vicinity of gladness and elation, but like a wisp of smoke, impossible to capture and easy to dissipate in the wind. Like me.

These days, I am not quite sure what brings me to the Window. I might be Peeking without even knowing it. Perhaps it's just being in recovery that does it for me. Perhaps it's in seeing how others do it. Maybe it's in working with others and availing myself to other alcoholics. I don't have hobbies per se; I don't have many interests

... what you see is what you get. I couldn't say that about myself in the drinking days. My duplicity ran deep, as did my resentments.

Exactly what brings me utter joy is something that I am still discovering. Perhaps it isn't a *thing* I do, like gardening or hula hooping or skydiving, but a state. I don't live in joy every moment of my life, but I do live in gratitude for most of it. Perhaps that is my Peeking. Perhaps there is something I have still yet to be given guidance to come upon. I don't know.

And I am okay in that "not knowing" right now. I am content to continue watching others Peek Through Joy's Window and see their total abandonment of self to pure joy and utter completion for that briefest of moments. I am content to watch my sons run and chance upon life and laugh and watch my wife coddle them and fuss over the dog ... her joy.

More will be revealed.

Time Out

Tokio (Munro 2009)

My alcoholism wants to kill me.

It puts me in ambulances and hospital beds and makes my family and friends think about funeral locations. Vodka bottles lead to hanging intravenous bags. Nurses and doctors with sad eyes take blood and give me back bloodwork that says I'm going to have a heart attack or stroke within 12 hours.

Yep, my alcoholism wants me six feet under. It has made that clear every time I relapse. And I say relapse and I don't say slip. Because where my alcoholism comes from a slip is something you do on ice or wear under a dress.

When I pick up a drink I'm not right back where I started … that would be a luxury … when I pick up a drink after not drinking, it's like I never stopped drinking. Weird how that works … deadly too.

But there are some things that have to happen before I pick up that drink.

First, my alcoholism has to get me alone. Preferably with a resentment. Resentments are like candy to my alcoholism. It just can't resist and it doesn't mind taking any from strangers.

So give me a resentment and get me alone and my disease locks the door and refuses to answer when anything that looks like a program of recovery comes knocking. It turns up the volume on the chaos so sounds of serenity can't be heard. It gives prayer and meetings and my sponsor and my higher power "the finger."

You see, my alcoholism is childish and resents the daily time out it gets when I do the things that keep me sober. My alcoholism wants to play only with me, whisper in my ear, share its big plans for us to fix the world and all its screwed up people, and make the ones who hurt us pay … my alcoholism wants me all to itself and loves when my program takes a nap or leaves the rooms.

So "I" have to make sure I become a we. I can't fight "cunning, baffling, powerful" alcohol alone. It's too big ... this fatal solution that is so sexy and dramatic and advertised everywhere ... but it's not on the breath of my friends in the fellowship or on their shirts or on the walls of where they hang out.

So I need to go there and hang out with them and laugh with them and call them and text them and do service with them. And now that I've been sober a bit, I can travel and have found thems all over the world that help me keep my face in the sun and put my alcoholism in its place.

Painting my Life with Colour

Kim R. (Munro 2013)

One year sober and my heart is filled with gratitude for all of the counsellors at Renascent who showed me through their own experiences the spiritual program of Alcoholics Anonymous — my "seed planters."

When I walked through the doors of the Graham Munro Centre, I knew that I was powerless over alcohol, but I had no idea that my life had become unmanageable as a result of my drinking. These counsellors drastically changed my perceptions about the nature of my disease. I was told that I had a soul sickness and that if I straightened out spiritually, I would straighten out mentally and physically as well. I was incredibly terrified and I felt as though I was destined to be broken, always.

Gradually, my design for self-destruction was pulled away in small pieces through the convictions of those powerful women. I borrowed their faith in the program. They believed in me when I could not even muster up an ounce of hope for myself. I certainly was not the same when I walked out of those doors 21 days later — the seed of sobriety had been planted. And I began to believe that my life could possibly be better if only I could stay sober.

I have been blessed with incredibly strong sponsorship and, as it turns out, getting sober was the "easier" part. Recovery was never sugar-coated for me. I was told that it was going to be difficult and that certain aspects of my life would seemingly feel worse before they felt better and that was good advice. I had dismissed the reality of my life entirely.

The real culprits were not my past or the people surrounding me — the real culprits were my disease of alcoholism and my inability to accept responsibility for who it was I had, in fact, become. I was imprisoned by alcohol, a slave to my bottles and had an unrelenting obsession that I could one day control my drinking. This was the illusion of my addictive mind; one that I believed time and time again.

One year ago, I could not envision staying sober for an entire day.

One year ago, I was completely broken on the inside.

One year ago, I thought the only thing that I had going for me was getting drunk.

One year ago, I could no longer endure being me.

One year ago, I felt absolutely worthless and undeserving of love.

But, I was desperate for a solution.

Today, I am learning to live from the inside out. I can love a lot and be loved. I can feel and I can share my feelings. And I can finally start to let go of some of the shame that never actually belonged to me to begin with. Sobriety still feels surreal for me on most days because I conditioned myself to "enduring" life. Now I am learning how to be me and that has been an amazing gift.

But most importantly — I can help others. I can be a seed planter too! I can share my life story in front of people. I can look people in the eye. I can find value in my past experiences and strength in my weaknesses. I can breathe for the first time. This is the journey that you helped me to find — and I am incredibly grateful to be able to see life with shimmers of colour.

Renascent changed the lens with which I view the world and gave me the opportunity to admit that alcohol had defeated me — and that is when I finally began to win at living.

I will never be able to find the perfect words to express just how Renascent has changed absolutely everything in my life. But I can strive to be that member of Alcoholics Anonymous who shows the newcomer this program. I want to promote the attraction of this program because that is what saved me from myself. The miracle of recovery is real.

As I continue to work and delve deeper into the causes and condition of my addiction, I know that the counsellors are always just a phone call away when I need them. Knowing that they are available keeps me on path and reminds me of how far I have come and how much further I can go if I let them help me.

To my Guardian Angel: Thank you for your donation because without the financial support I received, I may never have been able to get the help that I needed. My new life would never have been possible had it not been for you. I wish I could place my heart into your body, if only for a split second — just so you could experience what it feels like for me to be alive today. Gratitude.

Thank you for painting my life with colour.

About Renascent

Over the last 45 years, Renascent has helped more than 45,000 Canadians find hope and healing in recovery from addiction.

The Renascent Fellowship was founded in 1970 by Paul J. Sullivan and a group of businessmen, half of whom were recovering alcoholics, with the goal of opening a new type of treatment centre. Renascent's centre would be a 12-step, abstinence-based and gender-specific drug and alcohol recovery program.

On October 20, 1971, our first client, Donald, walked through the doors of Renascent. Tens of thousands of clients would follow him throughout the following decades.

The Renascent Foundation was incorporated in 1983 to enhance funding for the treatment of alcoholism and drug addiction and ensure that no one would be turned away for lack of funds. With the support of the Foundation, Renascent began to offer programs for families whose loved ones struggle with the illness of addiction.

Today, Renascent owns and operates four centres: the Paul J. Sullivan Centre for men in Brooklin, the Punanai Centre for men in Toronto, the Graham Munro Centre for women in Toronto, and the Lillian and Don Wright Family Health Centre in Toronto — home to our head office and family programs.

Still fiercely committed to 12-step, abstinence-based treatment, Renascent is changing the conversation about addiction and recovery in Canada. Renascent battles the family disease of alcoholism and drug addiction by helping the entire family, including kids. The largest residential treatment centre in Ontario, Renascent's treatment programs are trauma-informed and concurrent-capable; relapse prevention and family care services are available over the phone to ensure distance is never a barrier. Renascent was fully accredited in 2014, meeting standards of excellence assessed by external, non-biased reviewers.

Renascent offers immediate and affordable access to treatment within 24 hours. Donors, working together with our provincial funding partner (Toronto Central LHIN), safeguard public access for the 80% of Canadians who cannot afford treatment. At Renascent, we are passionate about the promise of recovery and we believe that recovery must be available for all who seek it.

24/7 Recovery Helpline: 1-866-232-1212

www.renascent.ca

Renascent
The road to recovery starts here.